SOME CORRECTIONS TO YOUR COPY OF

**HIDDEN PATTERNS:**
**POWER MONEY IN THE STOCK MARKET**

PAGE 23, SECOND PARAGRAPH:

"That was also a sell that missed the fall 1991 peak by only 12 percent" should be an independent sentence.

PAGE 60, TABLE 4-1:

Under 1992 the June 15 (Sell) 20 session results should be under a sub-head "to 6/30 buy".

TABLE 5-5, PAGE 87:

Has a section out of chronological sequence. The 12/85 ordinary sell, the 1/86 and 4/86 dip buys and the 3/87 and 7/87 short-term setup sells should precede the 11/87 waterfall buy.

PAGE 135:

Second paragraph reference to Chapter 2 discussion of "stoppers" should identify page 40.

PAGE 146:

The first sell listed for 8/82 at S&P 103.9 is a buy and should be in the buy column. The last sell should be dated 10/93.

# Hidden Patterns
*Power Money in*
*the Stock Market*

# Hidden Patterns

*Power Money in
the Stock Market*

Robert Kinsman

**IRWIN**
*Professional Publishing*
Chicago • Bogotá • Boston • Buenos Aires • Caracas
London • Madrid • Mexico City • Sydney • Toronto

| | |
|---|---|
| Marketing manager: | Angela Wells |
| Project editor: | Karen J. Nelson |
| Production manager: | Pat Frederickson |
| Designer: | Larry J. Cope |
| Art coordinator: | Kim Meriwether |
| Compositor: | Graphic Sciences Corporation |
| Typeface: | 11/13 Century Schoolbook |
| Printer: | The Maple-Vail Book Manufacturing Group |

**Library of Congress Cataloging-in-Publication Data**

Kinsman, Robert.
    Hidden patterns : power money in the stock market / Robert
Kinsman.
        p.  cm.
    Includes index.
    ISBN 1-55623-929-7
    1. Stocks.  2. Investments.  3. Speculation.   4. Business cycles.
I. Title.
HG6041.K56   1995
332.63'22—dc20                                                                94–24893

*Printed in the United States of America*
1 2 3 4 5 6 7 8 9 0 MP 1 0 9 8 7 6 5 4

# ACKNOWLEDGMENTS

Any major discovery and description of it requires the work of many people. This volume's subject is no exception. The list of participants in this effort would fill a page. Rather than burden this sheet, let me single out a few for special mention who have assisted in critical matters. Emory Richardson, a long-term client, mathematician and money manager, was invaluable in explaining and verifying the statistical support to the SPAR patterns, as well as working long enough with the advice generated by them to become a staunch advocate. Good friend, Zara Altair, deserves special thanks for use of her English Master's degree and financial expertise in critiquing the book's editing and for her steadfast support at moments when the project's finish seemed unattainable. Also deserving of unique thanks are the scores of clients who have worked with SPAR through the unfolding of its multiple facets during real time market events for the past three years. I truly could not have uncovered SPAR's scope without you.`

R.K.

# CONTENTS

# INTRODUCTION

Many investors believe that any stock market strategy which attempts to direct capital in and out of the market at opportune times is a timing strategy. Most investors inherently distrust timing. But, in comparison to a buy and hold strategy, these beliefs are conceptually true. The first is a definitional matter, the second a reflection of experience. The problem is, most timing methods attempt to identify relative market highs and lows within some time frame through use of a group of external market indicators and to direct capital in and out on that basis. This is theoretically almost impossible over time or the market would not be efficient. That's why so many timing systems eventually fail.

The strategy I'll discuss is neither buy and hold nor true timing. I call it a positioning strategy because it keeps investors on the long term, right side of the market. It does so with a set of patterns inherent in the market itself. The patterns have existed for nearly a quarter of a century, perhaps longer. They were discovered, not created. They aren't superimposed on the market nor are they comprised of a series of indicators that are supposed to say certain things. With the patterns the market itself is offering something never before seen: a series of repetitive measures of New York Stock Exchange (NYSE) breadth that appear at highly opportune times. Some occur at excellent times to buy, others when selling is smart. But they do not attempt to pick market highs or lows or advise when to get in or get out. In all, they are just great "pitches"

to hit. They represent power money moving in the market. We'll see why that money is worth our attention.

The following pages contain two key elements: (1) The discovery itself—a series of eight precise, repetitive patterns that appear in market breadth. I'll tell you what they are and how to recreate them. (2) A system developed to maximize the patterns' profits. The system is comprised of four separate modules, any of which can be used with any others. It is the patterns that are the system's centerpiece. They are unusual because of their computer-analyzed precision and repetitive results. Once these are known, any market professional can build a system to utilize them. Use my system, use your own or interchange them.

Critical to making a market strategy work profitably time after time—in addition to having a basis that is market inherent—is an understanding of the strategy's limitations. Here, they are modest. The patterns have a 94 percent accuracy for almost 25 years, not 100 percent. In aggregate, they have less than one chance in 1,000 of appearing randomly, not zero chance. They appear on average three to four times a year, not every day.

If you understood these limitations and a few others, as I used the patterns over nearly four years in real-time, you would have been (1) an aggressive buyer during October–November 1990 and again at the start of the Persian Gulf War in January 1991. (2) You would have taken some profits two days before the Soviet coup in August 1991, and

(3) bought aggressively three days before the Federal Reserve cut the discount rate a full percentage point in December 1991. (4) You also would have added aggressively to positions just after the half-year market slide ended in June 1992, and then (5) gradually taken profits on three occasions during the modest market rise of 1993 so that your last sale price was within 3 percent of the record highs of January 1994. And if your portfolio was as conservatively structured as mine in 1993, you would have beaten the market's total return by 12 percent. Most importantly, you would have understood that in using these patterns then or in the future, you would have about a 94 percent chance of catching *every* market move greater than 5 percent to 6 percent.

If you can live with these limitations, you have much to gain from the following pages, in part because buying and selling when the patterns appeared since May 1972 beat the S&P 500 by more than four to one while being invested in the S&P 500 only three-quarters of the time. That might happen again but don't quote me.

**Robert Kinsman**

*Editor's Note*
The closing date for this manuscript was January 31, 1994, at the record stock market high. The subsequent market decline is of course critical to results of the signals SPAR (stock pattern recognition) issued in 1993. The author has provided an important "1994 Update" in Chapter 8.

# Hidden Patterns

*Power Money in
the Stock Market*

# THE BASICS

# 1

# What Is SPAR?

Investors are constantly making "discoveries" about the stock market. At a relatively sophisticated technical level, many of these discoveries evolve into systems designed to beat the market. Their numbers are legion. Some of them even survive.

This volume details a discovery that substantively may well rank at or near the top among technical breakthroughs announced during my 30 years as a market professional. Major money movement—what I call "power money"—in the market repeatedly leaves recognizable patterns in market breadth. My term for the process that identifies the patterns is *stock pattern recognition* (SPAR).

The appearances of the patterns generate buy and sell signals on which investors can act with markedly profitable results—more than four times that of buying and holding the Standard & Poor's (S&P) 500. The patterns will be demonstrated by real-time use for nearly four years and back-tested results for another 18 years. The patterns are numerically derived and few in number—four on the buy side, four on the sell—and they frequently occur at the market's major highs and lows.

Computer analysis reveals SPAR patterns: first, the smoothed NYSE breadth trend, then that trend's maximum and minimum ranges over short term periods of one month or less. The computer program then compares the relationships of the trend ranges with their historic record. A buy or sell signal is generated when a historically repetitive, successful relationship appears.

Most important, these patterns are mathematically precise. When they occur, they fit algebraic formulas exactly to the specific days and numbers required; interpretation is unnecessary. The patterns either say buy or sell now, or they don't appear, a fact that makes them rare. Further, they may well represent the best available empirical evidence that the long-argued random walk theory in the stock market is definitively flawed, at least over certain time frames. SPAR is not random.

The following highlights SPAR's record from 1972 through 1993, including real-time use from the fall of 1990:

- 94.1 percent profitable (32 of 34) total buy–sell trades measured against the S&P 500, with never a down year and a gain of more than four times that of an S&P buy–hold, while invested only 75 percent of the time.

- No losing buy–sells for more than a decade; 20 consecutive profitable trades since 1982, when the loss was 0.25 percent in the S&P.
- A statistical accuracy termed the best possible—"highly significant"—by independent testing of all buy–sell and sell–buy trades, and trades to fixed dates of one, three, and seventh months, with a chance of being random ranging from one in 625 to one in 2 million. (See Statistical Notes.)
- Identification of 14 of the 15 major market highs and lows within an average of 3.6 percent of the precise levels.

With that sort of record, you may wonder how much of SPAR I'm willing to reveal. By the end of Chapter 2, I believe that the patterns will have been explained in sufficient detail for you to understand why and how they work and broadly how to recreate them.

## SPAR's Relationships to Other Technical Measurements

It's true that a large number of technical market "patterns" have been recognized, some of which boast fine records. In the broad sense, the advance–decline line itself is a pattern. So are measures of the high-low balance, market sentiment, the number of stocks above or below their 10-week and 30-week moving averages, and so forth. Chart analysis itself relies on repetitive patterns. Some of the more durable, if arguable, market theories are derived from patterns, including the Elliott Wave Theory and the Gann Method. Even computerized trading in baskets of stocks against their related futures contracts relies on patterns. Indeed, the latter's computer selection of correct conditions is generically closest to the way SPAR is revealed.

All told, about 100 technical market indicators have relied on patterns to assess market direction and have had some degree of success. Next are the theories and systems derived from these technical market indicators, not counting the numerous allegedly repetitive cycles that some technicians swear by, if not at. That's a lot of patterns. However, excluding computerized trading, nearly all of these indicators and theories based on patterns have one of two qualities in common. They must either be interpreted in some market context or be supported by other indicators. Few stand alone. Indeed, the major sales point of one prominent market technician is that it is the weight of the evidence of many indicators that provides the best market insight.

This is of course a fair point. The use of multiple indicators often provides valuable insight and successful recommendations, but that is clearly different than using SPAR. It stands alone, totally unrelated to anything the market or the economy or the political world is doing, (except insofar as those factors may be considered by the people moving major money that creates the patterns.) The patterns appear in bull markets, bear markets (though less frequently) and trading markets. When they appear, they require no analysis other than to distinguish a buy from a sell. Of course, we differentiate one type of pattern from another in terms of its relative historical reliability, and we quantify how aggressively to act on it based on outside market forces. But when a SPAR buy or sell signal pops on the computer screen, it inherently tells SPAR followers what they should do.

Probably the clearest distinction between SPAR patterns and the myriad other market indicators and apparent cycles is that SPAR patterns are not truly "indicators" at all. Instead, they describe precise events when they occur. I've taken them a step further and created an investment system around them. Think of the difference this way. A market indicator gives a continuous reading of one aspect of market conditions. With a moving average, for example, the market is either above it, below it, or on it. Each daily "read" says something about current market conditions. Never mind whether they are correct in calling the future trend. The current status is always knowable. It is the interpretation that may be in doubt.

SPAR patterns don't give continuous market readings. True, on the day they appear they reveal that power money has moved in or out of stocks in a way that in the past has altered market breadth.

But after those initial appearances, five days or three weeks or six months later, the pattern says nothing more until another SPAR pattern appears. It's also true that when SPAR signals a buy or sell, that mode continues in force until reversed. This is the way SPAR tells investors which side of the market to be on for months at a time. But SPAR doesn't time the market, offering frequent opinions about interim tops and bottoms. It speaks when it speaks and then is silent. Investors can assume the last comment remains in force.

Note two related points: (1) SPAR has been unusually accurate in appearing at *major* market tops and bottoms, but it does not ring the bell to identify them (see Table 1–2). (2) We can always look at market history in the light of a given pattern type and assess the probability that the market will move in a similar way in the future. In this sense, we have a steady read on the market. However, once the pattern has been acted upon, the value of this opinion diminishes as time and market conditions change. There is still no continuous opinion from any SPAR pattern. Therefore, I don't consider SPAR to be a true market indicator. The best term to describe it is *positioner*. It tells investors whether their overall action mode should be buying or selling. Timing is then left to other factors, two of which, short-term accuracy and the smoothed advance-decline (ADS) charts, we'll address in Chapters 5, 6 and 7.

## What are the Patterns?

Probably the best way to view the patterns is through an observation made by highly regarded investor Warren Buffett. He said investors in the stock market are like baseball batters who can wait as long as they like for the right pitch. SPAR patterns are very good indications of the right pitches. If you don't hit one when it's served up, you may have to wait quite awhile until the next. (The SPAR *system* also tells you when to be swinging for the fence and when not to be swinging at all.)

Some investors want to know what to do when *they* are ready. They want the continuous read. But that's the mark of an amateur. Experienced and professional investors know the stock market does what it wants when it's ready, not when they are. SPAR tells us when important market action is occurring. Its history says those are conditions upon which to act.

SPAR patterns aren't the whole system I use, however. I've taken them further because of two important elements of investing that the patterns do not reveal: (1) how hard to hit the pitches, and (2) what to do between the great pitches to become prepared for the next market move. In the first case, I've combined SPAR with unrelated market indicators to determine how aggressively to act upon the pattern signals. The other indicators are part of the simplified form of Stock Model I discussed in my book, *There's Always a Bull Market*.[1] Use of this model with SPAR is the subject of Chapter 3.

The second element is not one I added, but one that's inherent in the development of the SPAR patterns. This is the smoothed advance-decline data SPAR analyzes to discover its patterns. We see it in the form of a graph oscillator[2] that is susceptible to chart analysis and can quite successfully call the short-term market trends between SPAR pitches. This analysis gets extensive treatment in Chapter 6.

Thus, the SPAR system is made up of four elements or modules: the patterns themselves, information on how aggressively to act on them, short-term action timing on buys and sells, and market trend analysis. It is a complete approach to stock investing that even suggests the types of stocks to buy and sell in given market trends. But that gets us ahead of the SPAR story. Let me now be more precise about the nature of the patterns.

The pattern appearance record covers more than 5,500 trading sessions from 1972 through 1993 on the NYSE composite tape, including regional exchange trades. Economic conditions during that period included four recessions, major inflation, the longest peacetime expansion on record and disinflation. Those years also cover seven bear markets of 15 percent or more, including a major Crash, a wide trading range of two years, two major bull markets, and the flat markets of late 1991 through 1993.

Through all this, our Pattern Recognition computer program and another program from NAVA Development of Lewiston, New York, discovered only eight consistent patterns that appeared repetitively and successfully. The programs rejected scores of patterns that either occurred infrequently or weren't reliable in producing profits in the S&P 500. Of course, one could track data on market history further back than two decades. However, as we'll see shortly, these patterns

---

[1] *There's Always A Bull Market*, by Robert Kinsman, Homewood IL: Dow Jones-Irwin, 1990.
[2] In market technicians' language, an oscillator is a graph line that swings regularly or irregularly from positive to negative levels and back.

arise primarily from institutional activity. Prior to the 1970s and even into the 1980s, this activity was not the force in the market that it has become since. Indeed, successful patterns did not appear as frequently in the 1970s and were less precise than in the 1980s–90s, although there may be several reasons for this.

What's more, our starting point in 1972 was near a market high, as was the case at the time of this writing, so our results are biased as little as possible by the 1974–93 bull market. See Appendix I for a complete list of all pattern signals and track record calculations.

## Statistical Summary

The four SPAR buy patterns occurred a total of 34 times since mid-1972. One appeared only five times because it is triggered solely by fast market declines of 14 percent or more. The remaining 29 appearances were split between the three other types of buys: 13, 8, and 8 times. Tracked to the first sell signal in sequence thereafter, only two were unprofitable, the worst of which was –0.25 percent in the S&P 500 in 1982.

The four sell patterns appeared a total of 49 times: 25, 16, 5, and 3 times. However, the 25 most frequent appearances came from one pattern that identifies only the ends of market rallies and does not automatically issue a sell signal. I call it the "stopper" and it is informational only. Twenty-four sell patterns are thus trackable. As one would expect in the generally rising market of the past two decades, the success rate of the other three sell patterns is lower than the buy patterns: Five appearances were unprofitable at the next buy signal and three have unknown results at this writing. Thus, 16 of 24 sells were profitable at the following buy signal. In total, the trackable action patterns were profitable on 48 of 55 occasions and unprofitable on 7. Using the standard chi-square test for stocks, this is statistically a "highly significant" record.[3] Specifically, it has far less than one chance in 1,000 of occurring at random. This alone amply states the point that SPAR has uncovered a most significant phenomenon.

When I tracked SPAR against the S&P 500 through the completed buy–sell pair on January 13, 1993, SPAR signals generated a portfolio gain of more than 1400 percent. That compares with a 339 percent gain for the S&P 500 buy–hold over the same period. (Dividends are excluded, but this benefited the S&P because SPAR was out of the market nearly 25 percent of the time during which the capital could earn interest at money market rates that were higher than the S&P yield.) See Table 1–1 for the track record.

Meanwhile, the buy-to-first-sell patterns produced the two losses, both in 1982:0.2 percent and 0.25 percent. However, in measuring all buys to all succeeding sells, a third loss occurred: the result of a fifth

---

[3]The chi-square test for stocks, courtesy of John McGinley of *Technical Trends* in Wilton, CT, based on tables created by Arthur Merrill.

**TABLE 1–1    SPAR 1972-1993 Track Record**

| Date | Pattern | S&P Index | Gain from First Buys to First Sells* |
|------|---------|-----------|--------------------------------------|
| Back-Tracked: | | | |
| **1972** | | | |
| May 12 | Thrust buy | 106.4 | |
| Sept. 1 | Setup sell | 111.5 | 4.8% in 3.5 months from 5/72 |
| Oct. 10 | Setup sell | 110.0 | |
| Year-end | | 118.1 | |
| **1973** | No patterns | | |
| **1974** | | | |
| Oct. 7 | Major buy | 65.0 | |
| Oct. 17 | Waterfall buy | 71.2 | |
| Dec. 10 | Major buy | 67.3 | |
| Year-end | | 68.6 | |
| **1975** | | | |
| Feb. 26 | Dip buy | 80.4 | |
| Apr. 10 | Major buy | 83.8 | |
| July 30 | Dip buy | 88.8 | |
| Dec. 4 | Dip buy | 87.8 | |
| Dec. 11 | Major buy | 87.8 | |
| Year-end | | 90.2 | |
| **1976** | | | |
| Mar. 16 | Dip buy | 100.9 | |
| Aug. 16 | Setup sell | 104.4 | 60.6% in 22.3 months from 10/74 |
| Dec. 14 | Long-term sell | 105.1 | |
| Year-end | | 107.5 | |
| **1977** | | | |
| Feb. 1 | Setup sell | 102.5 | |
| June 30 | Long-term sell | 100.5 | |
| Sept. 15 | Setup sell | 95.2 | |
| Year-end | | 95.1 | |
| **1978** | No patterns | | |
| **1979** | No patterns | | |
| **1980** | | | |
| Feb. 7 | Setup sell | 116.3 | |
| April 15 | Waterfall buy | 102.6 | |
| Aug. 29 | Dip buy | 122.4 | |
| Year-end | | 135.3 | |
| **1981** | | | |
| Mar. 25 | Long-term sell | 137.1 | 33.6% in 12.2 months from 4/80 |
| Oct. 14 | Waterfall buy | 118.8 | |
| Year-end | | 122.6 | |
| **1982** | | | |
| Jan. 28 | Thrust buy | 118.9 | |
| April 23 | Ordinary sell | 118.6 | (0.2%) in 6.3 months from 10/81 |
| Aug. 13 | Dip buy | 103.9 | |
| Aug. 16 | Major buy | 104.1 | |
| Year-end | | 140.6 | |
| **1983** | | | |
| June 2 | Dip buy | 162.6 | |
| Nov. 11 | Ordinary sell | 164.4 | 58.2% in 15 months from 8/82 |
| Year-end | | 164.9 | |
| **1984** | | | |
| Aug. 1 | Thrust buy | 154.1 | |
| Year-end | | 167.2 | |

**TABLE 1–1   SPAR 1972-1993 Track Record** *continued*

| Date | Pattern | S&P Index | Gain from First Buys to First Sells* |
|---|---|---|---|
| **1985** | | | |
| April 25 | Setup sell | 183.4 | 19.0% in 8.7 months from 8/84 |
| July 12 | Setup sell | 193.3 | |
| (July 19 | Long-term sell | 195.1 in same seq.) | |
| Aug. 8 | Dip buy | 189.0 | |
| Dec. 13 | Ordinary sell | 209.9 | 11.0% in 4.2 months from 8/85 |
| Year-end | | 206.9 | |
| **1986** | | | |
| Jan. 13 | Dip buy | 206.7 | |
| April 8 | Dip buy | 233.5 | |
| Year-end | | 242.2 | |
| **1987** | | | |
| March 19 | Setup sell | 294.1 | 42.3% in 14.2 months from 1/86 |
| July 29 | Setup sell | 315.7 | |
| (Aug. 7 | Setup sell | 323.0 in same seq.) | |
| Nov. 30 | Waterfall buy | 230.2 | |
| Year-end | | 247.1 | |
| **1988** | | | |
| Jan. 15 | Major buy | 252.0 | |
| Oct. 17 | Setup sell | 276.4 | 20.1% in 10.5 months from 11/87 |
| Nov. 30 | Thrust buy | 273.7 | |
| Year-end | | 277.6 | |
| **1989** | | | |
| Feb. 27 | Dip buy | 287.8 | |
| May 26 | Setup sell | 321.6 | 17.5% in 6.1 months from 11/88 |
| July 3 | Dip buy | 319.2 | |
| Oct. 31 | Major buy | 340.3 | |
| Dec. 20 | Dip buy | 342.8 | |
| Year-end | | 353.4 | |
| **1990** | | | |
| May 4 | Thrust buy | 338.4 | |
| July 12 | Ordinary sell | 365.4 | 14.5% in 12.2 months from 7/89 |
| Oct. 1 | Major buy | 314.9 | |
| <u>REAL TIME</u> | | | |
| Oct.26 | Waterfall buy | 304.7 | |
| Year-end | | 330.2 | |
| **1991** | | | |
| Jan. 17 | Thrust buy | 328.0 | |
| Aug. 14 | Setup sell | 389.9 | 23.8% in 10.5 months from 10/90 |
| Dec. 16 | Thrust buy | 384.5 | |
| Year-end | | 417.1 | |
| **1992** | | | |
| June 15 | Setup sell | 410.1 | 6.7% in 6 months from 12/91 |
| June 30 | Thrust buy | 408.1 | |
| Year-end | | 435.7 | |
| **1993** | | | |
| Jan. 13 | Setup sell | 433.0 | 6.1% in 7 months from 6/92 |
| Aug. 16 | Ordinary sell | 453.0 | |
| Oct. 28 | Setup sell | 467.7 | |
| Totals | | | |
| | Compound gain | 1,412.5% | |
| | S&P buy–hold | 339.6% | |
| | Average trade | 22.7% in 9.7 months | |

*Considers the first buy in a buy sequence to the first subsequent sell. Not to be confused with taking all buys to first sell or all buys to all sells. The different results are not statistically significant.

consecutive sell in 1977 arising from a fifth consecutive prior buy. In practice, this signal probably would not have been acted upon because an investor would likely have been out of the market after so many unbroken sell signals. (This is not shown because Table 1–1 covers only buys to the first sequential sell.)

Further, SPAR has had no unprofitable buy–sell trades since mid-1982; Table 1–1 shows 20 straight profitable trades. SPAR's patterns have also caught the major market highs in 1972, 1976, 1980, 1983, 1987, and 1990, and the major lows in 1974, 1980, 1982, 1984, 1987, and 1990. SPAR's poorest performance at these highs or lows was 7.8 percent early in September 1972, but that and its follow-up sell in October 1972 avoided the worst bear market of this generation, 1973–74. Moreover, the 15 signals closest to all those market highs and lows had an average miss of less than 4 percent. SPAR called the 1987 top within 4.1 percent and the low within 2.7 percent. (See Table 1–2. Appendix II has all signals tracked to fixed dates of one, three, and seventh months later.)

It should be clear that the breadth patterns I discovered are highly significant from the position of stand-alone independence, statistical assessment, and track record. It is fair to say that the patterns represent truly "smart money." The patterns shown in Table 1–1 are identified by their assigned names and will be discussed shortly.

## Why the Patterns Appear

The SPAR patterns are not mere numbers on paper. There are strong reasons for their existence. First, the big picture. NYSE-listed stocks now number in excess of 2,500 issues that trade on a given day. This includes nearly 1,000 issues with market capitalizations above $500 million and nearly 800 preferred stocks that are almost entirely "small cap." Another one-third of the trading issues can reasonably be considered secondary equities.

The breadth of the New York Stock Exchange matters because of its wide representation of large, medium, and secondary stocks. The NYSE has what counts when investors discuss "the" market. It follows that it is a logical place to look for patterns that affect the market. Moreover, the NYSE list wins by default. The American Stock Exchange has too few issues traded—about 700 per day—to be relevant. NASDAQ, the over-the-counter market, has nearly 5,000 daily trades, but the difference between the numbers of gainers and losers on most days is modest. 15 percent net move one way or the other is almost a stampede.

### Power Money

Only three categories of market measurements are able to describe broad market movements: breadth, trading volume, and the indexes. Breadth measures the number of issues changing price but not the amount of price change, so it is logical to compare breadth with an index that measures the size of price change. Contrary to popular belief, however, it is the troops that lead the generals in almost every battle; that is, the net breadth number is more critical than the size of changes in spotting developing trends. While this does not detract from volume as an important market indicator, perhaps in combination with breadth and an index, breadth alone is highly significant. Hence, my search for reliable, repetitive patterns in NYSE breadth.

Breadth changes also must occur because of the movement of truly large amounts of capital. This means institutions and other massive sources of capital—power money—are the principal contributors.

While there is no precise way to measure the amount of money required to change the market's advance–decline breadth, there's no doubt it is sizable. For example, take two days, Friday, February 5 and Monday, February 8, 1993. On the 5th, 89 more issues gained than declined on the NYSE. On the 8th, net gainers totaled 21, or 68 fewer net gainers than on the 5th. Total volume up and down was 210.6 million shares on February 5, and 249.4 million on February 8, a net increase of 39.2 million, which arose from an increase in net downside volume. Obviously, not all of the downside volume went into the 68 fewer net gainers. If we assume that 10 percent of the volume went into losers, and assign a low average share price of $25, nearly $100 million was involved. That came from a small net advance-decline change. A typical day sees net changes of 200 or more from the prior day. When we speak of advance-decline changes involving hundreds of millions of dollars, that's not Aunt Tillie's cookie-jar money we're talking about. Only institutional money is of that magnitude.

The term *institutional money* is too narrow. Does institutional money include that of NYSE specialists, floor brokers, independent market makers, and computerized program traders? What about derivative product traders and managers of trading portfolios such as private hedge funds? They surely contribute, perhaps heavily, to breadth changes, but aren't thought of as institutions.

I use the term *power money* to include all large capital sources that can't precisely be termed institutions, as well as the pure institutions we know such as banks, insurance companies, and mutual funds. All we need recognize is that power money represents huge sums of capital, and it is that capital that affects market breadth most directly.

Moreover, numerous studies have confirmed that the market has become increasingly institutionalized. In 1992, the Securities Industry Association revealed that institutions owned more than 50 percent of all shares outstanding, up from 40 percent in 1980, due largely to the flood of capital into mutual funds. NYSE studies indicate that institutional activity on that exchange accounts for over 70 percent of average daily volume. Thus, institutions that make up the bulk of the power money that moves market breadth have taken increasing control of market movements.

Power money acts in surprisingly few ways. First, when it moves, it must move large blocks of stock. The current definition of a *block trade* is 10,000 shares or more. Many trades are 50,000 to 100,000 shares or more. Block trades and related price-determined follow-up moves by traders and speculators have the clear potential not only to change market price, but also to turn a decline into an advance or at least to bring the session price to unchanged. Block trades can dramatically affect breadth, and power money must trade in blocks.

However, one well-known quality of power money activity is that it is adverse to price change. Power money attempts whenever possible to make its moves with the least price disturbance. The bull in the china shop doesn't need to break all the china. It just wants to move. Thus, power money often hides most of its activity in small or modest price changes, especially in large capitalization stocks. This means that little is known about the aggregate intent behind these trades. Of course, the number of blocks traded, overall trading volume, advance–decline balance, and the market averages reveal some things, but they can't explain the reasoning behind the activity or its methodology—interesting facts to know, to say the least. If some form of pattern for this market activity could be identified, more could be known. That's what I've done. SPAR says that when power money moves, follow it.

In my search for breadth patterns on the computer as a result of using smoothed breadth charts for a decade, I did not begin with the anticipated qualities just discussed and proceed to unearth patterns that fit. On the contrary, I looked for *any* patterns that repeated regularly at important turning points in the market and found out whether they also occurred repetitively at other profitable points. Then I checked the patterns against anticipated institutional actions. Each of the patterns has a practical reason to exist, based on widespread knowledge of how power money behaves.

Table 1–2 shows SPAR pattern results at their most dramatic. A SPAR signal has occurred within 7.8 percent of each of the 15 major market highs and lows since 1972 with one exception, the 1978 low when no buy signal appeared. The average shortfall was 3.6 percent. This is all

**TABLE 1–2   SPAR Record at Major Highs and Lows\*** (1972-1993)

| Actual High, Low | | Closest SPAR Signal | | |
|---|---|---|---|---|
| Date | S&P 500 | Date | S&P 500 | S&P Difference |
| H: Jan. 11 '73 | 120.2 | (S) Sep. 1 '72 | 111.5 | 7.8% |
| L: Oct. 3 '74 | 62.3 | (B) Oct. 7 '74 | 65.0 | 4.3% |
| H: Sep. 21 '76 | 107.8 | (S) Aug. 16 '76 | 104.4 | 3.3% |
| L: Feb. 28 '78 | 87.0 | None | | |
| H: Feb. 13 '80 | 118.4 | (S) Feb. 7 '80 | 116.3 | 1.8% |
| L: Mar. 27 '80 | 98.2 | (B) Apr. 15 '80 | 102.6 | 4.3% |
| H: Nov. 28 '80 | 140.5 | (S) Mar. 25 '81 | 137.1 | 2.5% |
| L: Aug. 10 '82 | 102.6 | (B) Aug. 13 '82 | 103.9 | 1.3% |
| H: Oct. 10 '83 | 172.6 | (S) Nov. 11 '83 | 164.4 | 5.0% |
| L: Jul. 25 '84 | 147.8 | (B) Aug. 1 '84 | 154.1 | 4.3% |
| H: Aug. 25 '87 | 336.8 | (S) Jul. 29 '87 | 315.7 | 6.7% |
| L: Dec. 4 '87 | 224.0 | (B) Nov. 30 '87 | 230.2 | 2.8% |
| H: Jul. 16 '90 | 369.0 | (S) Jul. 12 '90 | 365.4 | 1.0% |
| L: Oct. 11 '90 | 295.5 | (B) Oct. 26 '90 | 304.7 | 3.1% |
| Interim: Feb. 2 '94 | 482.0 | (S) Oct. 28 '93 | 467.7 | 3.0% |
| | | | Average | 3.6% |

\*Preceding S&P 500 moves greater than 15 percent.

the more remarkable because every SPAR pattern contributed to this record. Not shown: the occasions when more than one SPAR signal appeared at approaches to market highs and lows at 10 of the 14 signal occurrences. Single appearances came only with the February and November 1980 highs, the October 1983 high, and the July 1990 high. SPAR usually produces more than one pattern when power money is moving.

In sum, the SPAR patterns offer a highly valuable piece of information: When power money is moving in or out of the market, it moves in a way that disturbs market breadth in patterns that it has before.[4] These patterns are not statistically random, have been highly profitable to act upon, and have had a remarkable ability to occur near major market highs and lows. This information alone might be sufficient to have, but the total SPAR System goes on to provide frequent opinions about market trends and it colors the patterns to tell us how aggressively to act on them.

You have now seen what could fairly be said are SPAR's intriguing results. What about the "practical reasons" for the existence of the patterns? Too many observable market phenomena are neither supported by sound reasons to exist nor an adequate theory for being, and as a result must be suspect. SPAR is very well supported theoretically. Chapter 2 digs into this point and other critical topics such as, how do we move from track record to reality in the computer? And exactly how are the patterns seen? Figure 1-1 completes our picture of the SPAR record with a graph of all SPAR buy and sell signals from 1987 through 1993.

---

[4]The years 1992 and 1993 prompted a caveat to this. Power money rotated not only between industry sectors but also across broad market concepts like value versus growth investing. It is possible that the signals SPAR generated caught these movements in addition to those that were entirely in or out of the market. Is this a new phenomenon that will make SPAR less accurate? Not likely. Most long, relatively flat markets have displayed a similar sector rotation, such as most of 1976 and the last half of 1983. The bottom line is that the SPAR system has a means of dealing with this phenomenon in its readings of short-vs. long-term market trends.

**FIGURE 1-1   S&P 1987–1993 with SPAR Signals**

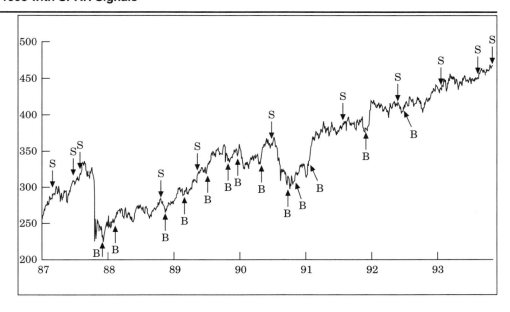

# Module One: Pattern Characteristics

The basis for the precise SPAR patterns is simply the NYSE net *daily* advances less declines, which are then smoothed with a front-weighted moving average. In Figure 2–1, line A shows the unsmoothed advance-decline (A–D) for early January 1992. Clearly it's a ragged plot. To better determine its trend, I have calculated line ADS (Smoothed Advance-Decline), the exponential moving average of line A-D. ADS is an oscillator that irregularly moves between positive and negative numbers and overbought/oversold levels. As such, ADS measures the momentum behind market breadth.

One important quality of this smoothing method is that it is self-correcting. Potential errors in ADS, even relatively large ones, are corrected within 30 to 40 trading days to less than one-tenth of a point. Any single error in the data is not long perpetuated in the database, while a front weighting to the current day is still achieved.

The key value of ADS is its frequent and startling ability to lead

**FIGURE 2–1   January 1992 NYSE Advance–Decline with Moving Average**

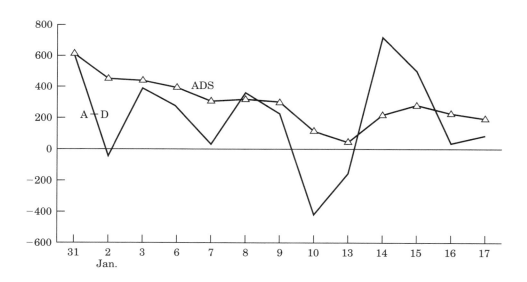

the trend in the S&P 500 Index. A good example can be seen by comparing the ADS in Figure 2–1 with the S&P Index in Figure 2–2. The ADS downtrend is the opposite of the S&P's modest rise. From market history, you'll recall that it was the S&P that turned down next, not matching the high shown for more than six months. As you will read in Chapter 6, this foreshadowing is an important quality to utilize between appearances of the actual SPAR signals.

Against this potential value, ADS has two bothersome characteristics: (1) It does not signal precise buy or sell points although it approximates them better than most oscillators do, and (2) it does not readily forecast the magnitude of market trends that it spots. However, ADS often allows us to forecast when a trend will begin and end, and to have that opinion accurate within a day or two. That's quite a lot to get from one chart, and although I used this capability with some success for a decade from 1981, imprecisions remained.

This inexactness was the genesis of SPAR. In the fall of 1990, I began working with a computer to determine whether ADS could reveal more than it did on the charts. I began by breaking down ADS into four components that better measured its continuing trends. It is in the relationships of these components to one another that the actual SPAR patterns appear. Figure 2–3 shows the four parts around one of SPAR's actual buy signals, December 16, 1991. It's a "thrust" pattern shown at the bar on the chart, and I'll return to it shortly.

The patterns were then perfected over the following nine months to the extent that I was able to offer them as part of my advisory service. I initiated a fax service utilizing SPAR exclusively in June 1991, and it has been in successful operation since. SPAR itself has nearly a four-year real-time track record, and the service has more than three years.

The SPAR patterns are dynamic. I often look for additional quali-

**FIGURE 2–2   January 1992 S&P 500**

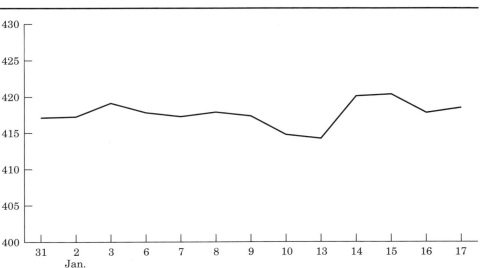

**FIGURE 2–3    December 1991 Thrust Buy**

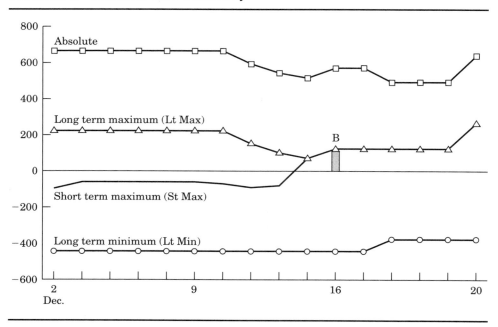

ties that will make them even more precise. In 1991 I discovered an extra ingredient for each sell pattern and one buy pattern that improved the quality of the calls. The most significant result was in the track record of 11 prior "ordinary" sells. Four patterns had a perfect record to the following buys with this one qualification, while the other seven without it saw five losses to the next buy dates. I naturally changed the formal definition of this and three other patterns with similarly discovered new qualities in my sample study period January 1, 1984–June 30, 1991. Pre-1984 and post-1991 patterns were not affected. This sacrificed some sample size, but the change in accuracy was dramatic.

Again, in the fall of 1993 I discovered two completely new patterns thanks to the new pattern recognition computer program acquired from NAVA Development Company. Where previous patterns were largely discovered by trial and error, a systematic method for identifying and tracking patterns was now available. The results were dramatic: the major buy pattern listed in Table 1–1 and the one I've named the "stopper" for its uncanny ability to spot the end of market rallies. (It's the informational pattern mentioned on page 10.) Additional patterns may possibly be discovered in the future. However, I believe it is highly unlikely that the present patterns will cease to function.

Related to this point is the so-called program trading and its impact on SPAR. I have said that program trades were generically the closest in methodology to the SPAR patterns, meaning that they are similar to one another in being generated by computer programs and in requiring little or no judgment prior to action. Few other technical patterns share these qualities. Most have either interpretive rules associated with them or require judgment on action timing. I do not mean that program trading and SPAR patterns are in any way similar in construction or dates of occurrence. In this sense, there is no relationship between the two sets of patterns.

The objective of program trading is also different from that of SPAR patterns. In its most common form, program trading is an arbitrage. It seeks a mathematical difference between an index futures price and its underlying "basket" of stock prices that can be locked in by simultaneous action in both. In its less widely used form following its October 1987 failures, program trading is a hedging of existing portfolios through the sale of index futures against them.

SPAR patterns don't seek or create arbitrage situations but simply identify power money movements that historically have been worth joining. Whether the movements arise from arbitrage, hedging, or anything else, SPAR must take all trading into account in generating its patterns. Thus, to the extent that program trading has been identified at all by SPAR patterns, the impact—as evidenced by SPAR's track record—has been positive.

Since the advent of program trading as a market force in 1984–85, SPAR patterns have generated no buy–sell losses, but the patterns have appeared more frequently. In the 12 years from 1972 through 1983, SPAR identified 28 valid patterns. But in the 10-year period, 1984–93, SPAR saw 32 patterns. Thus, SPAR became somewhat more active at the same time as program trading, whatever their methodological differences and similarities. (See Statistical Notes, Part I for a discussion of increased numbers of stocks traded as a reason for these additional pattern appearances.) Given all the facts, I would not expect to find, and have not, a specific buy or sell pattern for program trading. This leads to an interesting point. Since program trading in its various forms is among the most important, if not the greatest, change in the way power money functions in the market since the great popularization of mutual funds in the 1960s—a change that has had little effect on SPAR pattern appearances—it seems likely that it will take a development of even greater scope than program trading to affect our patterns in the future. Meanwhile, there's money to be made.

# How Power Money Buys

What sort of power money buying activity should we expect to find in daily market breadth? What sorts of qualities are common to power money "buy" action in the market? Do sound reasons exist for the patterns to appear?

# Herd Instinct

We know from both experience and financial press comment that a herd instinct exists among institutions. Despite power money's adversity to price change, its greed impulse is strong. Thus, strong buying should appear periodically just after the market begins to move higher, but before prices move too far. It also should arise suddenly and it should not appear at an exact market low. If the latter two qualities were present, it wouldn't be driven by a greed impulse. There's nothing to feel greedy about at market lows, but watching prices steadily rise without apparent reason does trigger that emotion. Thus, we should expect to find this "bandwagon" quality in the breadth patterns.

# Bargain Hunting

Another quality derives from the instinct almost opposite to that of the herd: bargain hunting. A key goal of most stock buyers, and power money is no exception, is to identify an attractively priced stock before it moves or when it's just beginning to move. The attraction may be "value," it may be a technical reaction to recent price action, or it may be news oriented. The common thread is that many stocks will be down in price on dips, or if up, they won't be far up. Clearly, this bargain-hunting quality is also a phenomenon to seek in market breadth.

# Adverse News

A third quality that market experience says should be present is power money action on adverse news. This news must be sufficient to move the entire market sharply and quickly lower but not change its fundamental (or technical) attractiveness. Waiting buyers suddenly find attractive prices that didn't recently exist, and they act on that condition. The Soviet coup of August 1991 is one example, the U.S. military move into Panama in December 1989 is another. If a single pattern exists under these conditions, it is certainly a worthwhile pattern to discover.

# End of Market Declines

A fourth power money buying quality occurs within a relatively short period of time in the aftermath of a relatively fast and steep downward move by the market. However, it is longer in duration than the adverse news spike. Such a pattern would identify valid bargain hunting that should occur after substantive market downswings that have some longevity, such as the typical end to a bear market. The theory supporting this quality is that power money looks not only for good values in stocks following serious declines, but also for signs that the market has stabilized and no further plunge seems to be developing. This takes both time and equilibrium. The periods of late 1974, mid-1982, summer 1984, fall 1987, and fall 1990 are examples of circumstances where this quality should be found.

Certainly, other potential buying qualities and theories could be explored, but I've shortened the list to four because, with one exception, they identify buying patterns I've found. It is unnecessary to identify all possible theoretical patterns in order to know that certain ones do appear, but we do need to ensure that the patterns that appear are based on sound reasons and are reliably repetitive. Theory must accompany evidence.

# The Inner Workings

Let's look at Figure 2–3 to dissect the smoothed advance–decline (ADS) numbers to see what their four component lines measure. LTMIN, the lower line, identifies the *minimum* level ADS has reached over the period of 20 trading days. Line LTMAX measures the *maximum* level ADS reached over the same period. STMAX changes the time measurement of the maximum to the most recent five trading days—very short term. The absolute line is the absolute result of subtracting LTMIN from LTMAX. It was created to eliminate minus numbers in the pattern formulas. These lines provide four simple measures of the ADS range over two different time frames, which is sufficient to reveal important action patterns.

The key question is how do the relationships between the movement of these components reveal critical market trends? Answering that took many months of analysis and reanalysis, and only eight of the relationships proved historically significant: the SPAR patterns.

## Finding The Patterns

As I began analyzing the components of the ADS oscillator, the first point to become clear was that they must have important reversal levels. Oscillators always do or they wouldn't oscillate; so should their parameters. The question was whether the levels were specific or a general range. I found both. The ADS line has general reversal areas above +300 and −300, as we'll see in Chapter 6. But the absolute line is more precise. I found that when it rose above one level after having been below it 20 days earlier, power money buyers often could be expected to act. When it fell below another level, sellers were likely to move.

At first glance, these qualities seem contrary to power money's intent to buy low and sell high. These conditions require buying higher and selling lower. But remember that the Absolute line is an absolute number resulting from a subtraction. Suppose that LTMAX upticked to +200 from +185 in one day, while LTMIN remained unchanged at -360;

that is, the maximum level ADS reached in 20 trading days increased that day, but the minimum 20-day level remained unchanged. That caused the buy precondition to be met as Absolute rose above a level that market history shows as critical: +550. It also revealed a solid net uptick in breadth, which you will see is a quality of the "thrust" buy pattern. (Also see Statistical Notes, Part I for the effect of increasing trading activity on pre-condition levels.)

The same reading also could arise from a *downtick* in LTMIN to, say, −375, while LTMAX remained unchanged at +185. That would produce the same crossover at 550 as above, but it reveals a solid downtick in breadth, which is needed for the buy pattern I call the "dip". Thus, either of these conditions (with refinements) presents a valuable piece of information, a positive absolute line crossover above 550.

The only other relationship among the lines that can produce this buy precondition occurs when both LTMAX and LTMIN move in the same direction simultaneously, but by different amounts so that the absolute line upticks. This uptick is simply a variation on the two previous interactions because when both lines move in the same direction and Absolute is up, either LTMAX must be up or LTMIN must be down. Since no other movements of LTMAX and LTMIN will create the right circumstances for this precondition, SPAR has found a significant limitation in the market conditions that create successful buys. Successful, because those conditions were present when all 34 buy patterns appeared, 32 of which were profitable at the first sequential sell.

When these facts are coupled with the ability of ADS to foreshadow broad market moves, we see that while two of the four possible buy preconditions are upticks in breadth, by no means does the broad market have to be rising and, in fact, it often is not. You can analyze for yourself the circumstances by which the absolute line produces a *decline* through any second set level for a sell precondition. They also are few.

A potential flaw in these buy and sell preconditions is that preset levels are used at all. What if Absolute reaches to only one or two numbers on either side of the preset? Or, why can't absolute reach differing levels depending on other market conditions? The answer to the first question is that close is indeed close and that fact should be theoretically considered in whether to act on a near-signal. But, SPAR's history shows no occasions when a miss of even three points occurred. Recall also that these numbers are preconditions and further relationships must be met to create a valid buy or sell pattern. And, these preconditions work; therefore, the valid criticism of the turning point numbers is that they conceivably could miss *other* profitable buys or sells. To that I again say that I have been unable to find other preconditions that are repetitively successful. If they do exist, consider that it is not necessary to identify *every* good pitch. Identify and hit only those that have high reliability for success.

As to the second question, I have adjusted the formulas for increased trading activity per Statistical Notes Part I. Moreover, SPAR is not attempting to identify a wide range of good or pretty good conditions that might signal profitable actions. SPAR seeks those conditions that have always or nearly always worked in all types of markets. Is it conceivable that other conditions have worked intermittently, or that other conditions will work in the future? Certainly. Is it likely that the SPAR patterns will cease working in the future? If you consider the theoretical and practical changes that are needed in the ways power money moves, the past statistical success of the patterns through all types of market conditions, and the failure of even a major change in power money actions, program trading, to disturb these patterns, the answer must be that it is extremely unlikely that SPAR patterns will cease to work.

## THE ACTUAL PATTERNS: BUYS

**Buy Track Record**
(*17 Patterns Rejected as Invalid*)

Buys to First Sells: 32 of 34 Profitable
Buys to All Sells, Same Sequence: 31 of 34 Profitable
To One Month: 29 of 34 Profitable
To Three Months: 29 of 34 Profitable
To Seventh Months: 31 of 34 Profitable

I've noted the existence of four consistent buy patterns over the past two decades and the reasons power money caused them. How are they measured?

# The "Thrust" Buy

The pattern I've called "thrust" is power money's equivalent of climbing on the bandwagon before it rolls away. This happened recently the day after the Persian Gulf War began, January 17, 1991, four days before the Federal Reserve Board cut the discount rate by a full percentage point on December 20, 1991, and two days before the Fed cut that rate by another half point on July 2, 1992. On those specific days, SPAR spotted the correct conditions during a time window when the buy precondition noted above existed.

On the first day of the precondition window, the 20-day maximum of smoothed breadth rose, revealing underlying market strength irrespective of the trend in the market averages. When this event occurred at or near the beginning of a meaningful overall breadth movement, it identified a pattern that had appeared successfully eight times in our 20-year span. Translated into Figure 2–4, component LTMAX rose that day, taking the absolute line up with it. Movement of STMAX and

**FIGURE 2–4   June 1992 Thrust Buy**

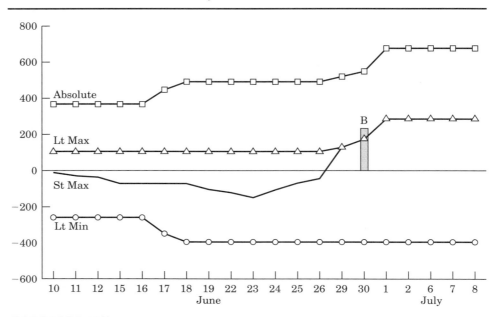

LTMIN are irrelevant to this pattern although STMAX, as a shorter measure of the maximum, would also be up that day.

As noted, these conditions have been met a total of just eight times in the past two decades, all of which occurred at the beginning of realistic breadth moves, including the 1991 and 1992 dates above. These were the thrust buys. A total of 14 additional thrust signals were rejected because they lacked one additional quality—the need for the breadth upswing to begin from a sufficiently low level. One loss was generated by this pattern at the next SPAR sell, but it was only 0.2 percent. Thrust gains have been somewhat smaller than the other buy patterns, with an average +10.8% percent in the S&P 500 at the first subsequent sell in the same sequence. Chasing stock rallies is the least preferred strategy so far as SPAR's breadth measures are concerned.

It may seem surprising that such simple conditions were met so few times in over 5,500 trading days, but it's true. Only 0.35 percent of all trading sessions qualified as thrust buys, of which only 31.5 percent met the rebound starting point condition. By analyzing the conditions closely, you'll see they are indeed highly restrictive. The precondition alone limits opportunities to an average of less than about a half dozen periods a year. Finding a 20-day high in smoothed breadth within them is clearly rare even on a random basis.

Perhaps more surprising is that each of the strong thrust pattern appearances occurred when the S&P 500 was down within the prior two weeks. None came after significant—more than 5 percent—up moves in the S&P had occurred from an interim low. This pattern is clearly a bandwagon clamor taking place just as important breadth moves begin. Among the thrust pattern's more notable successes were those of August 1, 1984, which saw a gain of 19.0 percent to the first sell pattern of April 25, 1985, and that of December 16, 1991, which at the January 13, 1993 sell, showed a gain of 12.6 percent, both measured in the S&P 500.

Another success was the Persian Gulf War start-up thrust buy at the close of January 17, 1991, when "everyone" said they were bearish, but the market had roared ahead more than 4 percent in two days. By the August 14, 1991, pre-Soviet coup SPAR sell, the S&P 500 gain was 18.9 percent, or 2.4 percent per month that was also a sell that missed the fall 1991 peak by only 2 percent.

---

**Thrust Pattern Record**

*(14 Patterns Rejected as Invalid)*

To next sell: 7 of 8 profitable, average 10.8% gain in 6.9 months

To one month later: 7 of 8 profitable

Three months later: 7 of 8 profitable

Seventh month later: 6 of 8 profitable

---

Many other apparent bandwagon moves began during the past two decades. Some of them went on to become decent market rallies, but the majority failed and only the right conditions produced consistent success. SPAR's thrust pattern found those conditions were sufficient despite their apparent simplicity.

# The "Dip" Buy

Contrary to the thrust pattern's relatively simple terms, the pattern I've named the "dip" is highly complex.

- It requires 11 different tests in its computer formula.
- It has appeared 13 times over the past two decades with 13 profitable results measured against the first sell in the same sequence.
- It produced no rejected signals.
- It generated zero losses at the three-month mark.

The only sequential loss came from its March 16, 1976, appearance measured to a fifth straight sell on September 15, 1977, some 5.6 percent on the S&P. The dip pattern's average gain is a healthy 19.1 percent to its first sell in sequence.

Recall that this pattern is theoretically identifying days when NYSE breadth is near its recent low, and it is beginning to show its first signs of strength—but not broad strength similar to the thrust pattern. Figures 2–5 and 2–6 are two highly successful examples of the dip pattern.

**FIGURE 2–5   July 1989 Dip Buy**

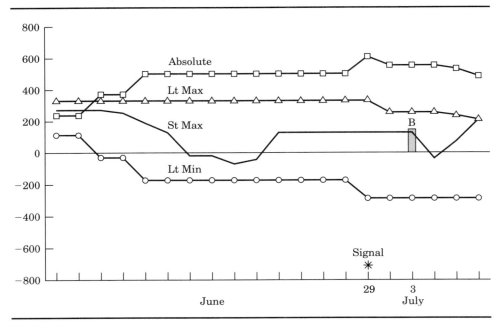

On the first day of the precondition, the dip pattern requires the 20-day smoothed breadth minimum (LTMIN) line to decline, taking the absolute level *up* with it. Then it requires the five-day maximum (STMAX) line to be either positive and at a week's high or equal to it, or that the *20-day* maximum (LTMAX) line be contrarily down that day. (The latter can occur when the 20-day minimum is falling, bringing the absolute combination up, while time runs out on the 20-day

**FIGURE 2–6   February 1989 Dip Buy**

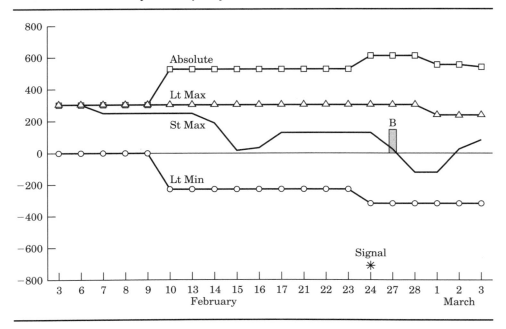

maximum, but the new 20th maximum day is not sufficiently below the previous 20th day to bring the absolute level down.) When these conditions are met, SPAR checks the absolute level to verify that it has not fallen in any of the prior eight days. Finally, the buy signal is triggered on the first up day in the S&P 500 after the tests are met. If the terms of the thrust pattern were restrictive while appearing outwardly simple, the dip is obviously highly restrictive even at first glance. Still, it produced some notable successes.

The dip pattern caught the August 1982 market bottom within two S&P points of the actual low and stayed with a 58 percent run to near the 1983 market high before a sell pattern appeared. It also spotted the December 1975 market pullback as worthwhile within one S&P point of the actual low, and rode it 18.9 percent to the August 1976 sell within three S&P points of 1976's market high—a peak that stood for three and one-half years. The dip pattern also identified the January 1986 backoff within 2 percent of its low, riding 42 percent to the ensuing sell pattern in March 1987.

The dip pattern had one unnerving ride with its December 1989 buy. It again succeeded in identifying a meaningful market easing, this time to within one-half an S&P point of the actual low, and it was immediately profitable with a 5 percent two-week run to the January 1990 high. Then the S&P plunged to a net 5.8 percent loss from the signal date at the January low. SPAR ignored the dive, and went on to generate a thrust buy pattern on May 4. That was prior to SPAR's most successful sell, July 12, 1990, only 1 percent and two days from an all-time high. The dip pattern's worst interim loss was 7.5% in August 1975, but it was again profitable by 17.6% at the next sell one year later.

---

**Dip Pattern Record**

Buy to first sell: 13 of 13, average gain: 19.1% in 8.7 months

To one month:10 of 13 profitable

To three months: 13 of 13 profitable

To seventh months: 13 of 13 profitable

---

# The "Waterfall" Buy

Some 18 percent below the 1990 market peak occurred the latest appearance of the shyest buy pattern, the "waterfall." This pattern is triggered only by steep S&P declines in relatively short trading periods, which are then followed by a period of stabilization. With this restriction, the waterfall has appeared only six times in the past two decades. Five of these appearances produced valid buy patterns with only one miniscule 0.2 percent loss from its October 1981 appearance. The sell that generated that loss on April 23, 1982, was also an excellent time to sell. The market plunged 12 percent in the next three months.

The average gain for the waterfall pattern's appearances is a hefty 25.8 percent. Note that such a small number of appearances carries an obvious potential caution with it.

This pattern's precondition is an S&P decline of 14 percent within 30 trading days, not the smoothed breadth numerical breach that the thrust and dip patterns require. However, the standard buy–sell numerical preconditions remain in force until the S&P decline reaches 14 percent. If the drop is lesser, the thrust or dip patterns might become operative.

Naturally, this introduces a risk. Might one of the two normal SPAR buy patterns appear on the way to a sizable S&P decline? This is possible in theory, but in practice the SPAR patterns have inherent protections. First, recall that the normal buy precondition requires smoothed breadth's absolute value to rise above its specified level. This occurs in only two ways during a sharp market decline: Either breadth must be moving strongly against the S&P 500 trend or it hits new lows along with the S&P. The first condition does not occur during sharp, fast S&P declines. The S&P is too broad an average to permit it (explaining one good reason why I use the S&P 500, not the Dow Jones Industrials, as my index.)

The second possibility is that the 20-day smoothed breadth minimum drops along with the S&P 500 Index. However, this automatically eliminates the appearance of the thrust buy pattern. It requires a *rise* in maximum 20-day smoothed breadth, not a decline in the 20-day minimum.

This leaves the dip and major buy patterns as the only practical possibilities to occur at the start of major market declines. With the dip, the possibility is less than remote. The dip pattern requires not only that the five-day maximum of breadth be positive and greater than or equal to its *weekly high*, but also that the absolute level not have a downtick in the prior eight sessions. The absolute qualification can be met, but how is the short-term maximum going to stay positive and hit or match its recent *highs* while the 20-day minimum is falling with a sharply declining S&P?

The only time it can do so is during the **five days** the short-term maximum reflects a recent peak, when smoothed breadth falls sharply enough to move the absolute line above its buy precondition. And this event must happen during **one day.** This is theoretically possible, but the window of opportunity is extraordinarily small and the fact remains that we are facing an incipient bear market. Not even the relatively fast-developing bear dives of late 1973, early 1980 (the fastest), 1987, and 1990 saw buy patterns as the bear swing unfolded despite their meeting the buy window preconditions. In fundamental terms, only a developing bear market that catches power money by surprise and on a rally (to drive the short-term maximum line up) qualifies. The SPAR patterns that reflect power money actions evidence exactly the opposite quality: SPAR was selling at or near every major market peak of the past 20+ years. I'll leave the potential occurrence of a major buy pattern in an incipient bear market to your analysis after I've illustrated the component qualities of the waterfall buy pattern below.[1]

An important methodological point now needs reemphasizing. SPAR patterns were discovered, not created. My research didn't attempt an exercise in logic to determine specific conditions that would fit all likely or even a few institutional trading activities. It went the other way around. I looked at the conditions that existed in smoothed NYSE breadth at important market turning points, developed the computer formulas that would recognize those conditions, and then tracked each formula through all the trading days in the 22-year time frame. The odds against a given pattern appearing at any point in time are as great as they are because the patterns themselves require stringent conditions, not because I thought they should. Those long odds should not be taken lightly, especially in the potential occurrence of a late buy pattern in a developing bear market.

Returning to the waterfall pattern, I observed the relationships between the four (ADS) components after the Crash of 1987 and the market break of 1990 (see Figures 2–7 and 2–8). Discovering that the conditions were the same with minor variations in both years, I then tested those terms on other important market breaks back to January 1984, modifying the conditions slightly so they encompassed the parame-

---

[1]Actually, the potential for a dip buy pattern to appear in a *slowly* developing bear market is greater than in a fast bear. So is the chance for a later sell pattern to appear at a higher level than the buy in the slow bear. This is a theoretical standoff.

**FIGURE 2–7    November 1987 Waterfall Buy**

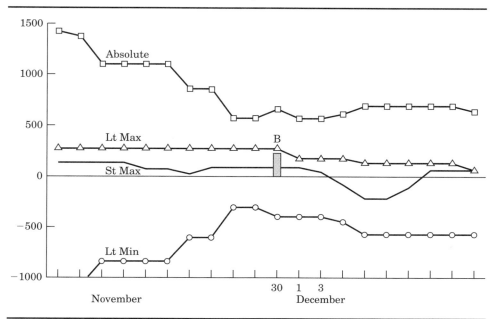

**FIGURE 2–8    October 1990 Waterfall Buy**

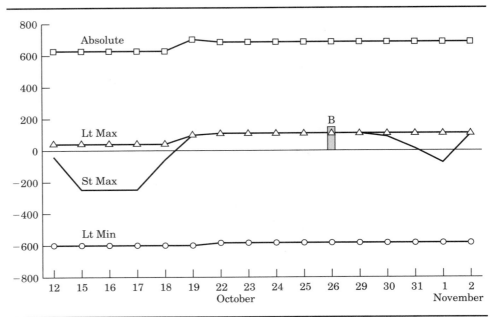

ters of all the periods. Then, to my surprise, these conditions successfully identified market lows in 1981, 1980 and 1974 without further change.

As I have stressed, the waterfall is the weakest buy pattern statistically because of its small sample, which in turn is caused by its need for a steep market decline in a short period. Prudence requires that the waterfall buy be acted upon with care, not with large amounts of capital, but this does not invalidate the pattern. Moreover, why did the waterfall correctly form a buy pattern extraordinarily close to each market low that it analyzed, but correctly reject the one in December 1973 that met the S&P drop condition and most of the remaining ones? Consider it extraordinary six-for-six luck; I have no statistical quarrel with that and am quite happy to work with that "luck" in the future.

Furthermore, the major buy pattern discovered in September 1993 has appearances that tend to confirm the waterfall buy. You will see in the next section that major buys in October 1974 and November 1990 came within two weeks of waterfall buys, leaving three of the five confirmed waterfalls standing alone.

What exactly does the waterfall pattern require? Figure 2–7 shows the ADS components following the famous Crash of 1987 with the buy pattern of November 30. The first requirement has already been noted, a 14 percent or greater decline in the S&P 500 from its high within 30 sessions. When that is met, the pattern looks for further conditions signifying developing market stability. One condition is that on the buy day the LTMIN line must be *above* its 20-day minimum, and that its level of four days earlier is less than or equal to the current reading. Then, the Absolute line must be at least 50 points above its minimum of the past 10 sessions, and the LTMAX line must exactly equal its level of four days earlier.

The two waterfall buys (see Figures 2–7 and 2–8) don't look alike. For example, in October 1990 the LTMIN line barely budges ahead of the buy. In November 1987, the LTMIN line moves up sharply and tails off, causing the Absolute line to decline, which it does not do in 1990. The formula allows for these variations. The correct conditions have been met. Appearances can be deceiving.

Still, these were tough conditions for smoothed breadth to meet. That's the point. Meeting them requires elimination of most "dead cat bounces," such as occurred immediately after Black Monday of the 1987 crash and the October 1990 lows. The pattern did catch an early rebound in October 1974, however, creating a temporary loss I noted earlier. With the gain of 36 percent to the July 1975 interim peak and the success the pattern enjoyed with the fast rebound of April 1980, the somewhat early call in 1974 can be forgiven, I think. Timing important market lows requires taking a variety of factors into account, and the waterfall pattern does that at the risk of being slightly early.

The small waterfall sample of five appearances is not the only warning that it must be handled carefully. My Stock Model usually raises the same caution. You will see in Chapter 3 that the model's short-term interest rate and market momentum components are likely to be negative during waterfall periods, which requires my model to issue cautious or outright bearish warnings too. When it does, it says don't hit any SPAR buy pitch aggressively.

Let's quibble further. If we take the eight appearances of the thrust buy pattern together with the five waterfalls, we have two of the four buy patterns with statistically modest numbers of occurrences. Does this call into question the validity of the whole SPAR buy sample size? No, it does not. The total buy sample remains a substantial 34 with only two errors to first sequential sells and only four to fixed dates. The waterall and thrust patterns aren't the weakest links in a single chain because each type stands alone and does not require the appearance of another type or succeeding types. It does suggest, however, that the rarer type patterns be treated with some wariness, which I do. Investing is not without risk. SPAR patterns have simply put that risk on a higher level of probability assessment.

---

**Waterfall Pattern Record**

*(1 Pattern Rejected as Invalid)*

To First Sell: 4 of 5 Profitable, Average 25.8% gain in 12.1 months

To All Sells, Same Sequence: 4 of 5 Profitable

To One Month: 5 of 5 Profitable

To Three Months: 4 of 5 Profitable

To Seventh Month: 4 of 5 Profitable

**FIGURE 2–9    October 1974 Major Buy**

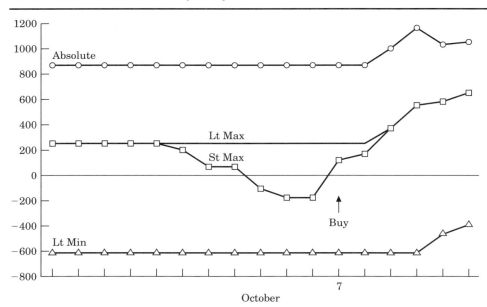

## The Major Buy Pattern

The major buy pattern was added to my list in 1993 with the help of the NAVA computer pattern recognition program. It is easy to view graphically, but it is complex algebraically, requiring 10 separate formula tests. It represents power money's bargain hunting urge.

**FIGURE 2–10    August 1982 Major Buy**

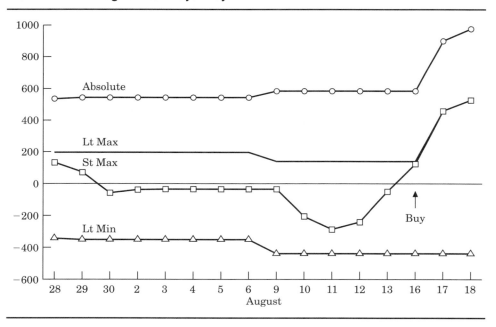

The major pattern is similar to the dip buy in that it looks for the market to have moved above a recent low but uses different criteria to identify it.

This pattern has the best long-range buy–sell record, with an average gain in eight appearances of 32.3 percent to the first succeeding sell patterns. The number of appearances is also reasonable and they produced no errors to the following sell. Since this pattern has not occurred since October 1990, its discovery has not altered SPAR's real-time record and did not taint my random sample with any alterations in it prior to 1984. The pattern appears successfully without reference to the usual pre-buy absolute level of 550 when (1) the S&P 500's high of the 13 prior sessions is at least 3.75 percent above its most recent five day low, (2) the previous day's ADS maximum, minimum, and absolute lines are each equal to those of five days earlier, (3) the short-term maximum line's lowest level of the current through previous 13 days is below the absolute line's highest level by a set amount in the same period, (4) the prior day's short-term maximum line is less than that of five days earlier, but the current day's level is greater than the day before, and (5) the current absolute line equals that of the previous day. When these characteristics are found, the absolute line is tested for a smooth up or down "stair-step" pattern that has no reversals in it.

---

### Major Buy Pattern Record

8 of 8 Profitable at First Sell, Average 32.3% gain in 14 Months.
One Month: 7 of 8 Profitable
Three Months: 7 of 8 Profitable
Seventh Month: 8 of 8 Profitable

---

# The Sell Patterns

Achieving successful sells during the past two decades was the acid test of any short-term or long-term market trading method. The great bull market of 1974–94 has seen to that. The difficulty of making successful sells into this bull charge is best seen by the brief periods in which any sell could have been successful.

If the Dow Jones Industrial Average is used as a market proxy and the measure of sell success is to pre-identify every down month since May 1972—the date of the first SPAR signal—only 96 months declined of a total of 248 months through 1993. That's 38.7 percent down. A sell call every month would have been wrong 61.3 percent of the time. Tough odds for sellers.

Against these conditions, SPAR is remarkable. Its sells were profitable against a five-week fixed hold on 18 of 24 tries for an accuracy of 75 percent, double that of the monthly sell odds. Moreover, six of those sells also came within a month of the *major* market tops of 1977, 1980, 1981, 1983, 1987, and 1990. Each of the three sell patterns participated in at least one call of those peaks.

---

**Sell Pattern Record**

(*27 Patterns Rejected as Invalid*)

To First Buys: 16 of 21 Profitable (3 incomplete)
To Five Weeks: 19 of 24 Profitable
To Three Months: 12 of 24 Profitable
To Seventh Months: 15 of 24 Profitable
The sharp decline in success at three and seventh months
reflects the market's propensity to rise over time.

---

## Expected Selling Characteristics

What do we know about institutional selling characteristics? What does experience tell us we should find in market action that is caused by institutional activity?

The obvious characteristic is that power money does not want to sell into down markets. It prefers to take its profits into rising markets because its block trades disturb prices less this way, and because power money rarely attempts to pick market highs, preferring to sell for other reasons such as overvaluation, technical patterns, etc. Our sell patterns should thus reflect rising markets in general, and increasing breadth in particular.

Moreover, net breadth increases can come from short-term, medium-term, or longer-term accumulations and they can parallel the market averages or not. Some discrimination concerning these factors should be present in the patterns. In addition, whether the market has come off a recent low in its current upswing has some import because a brief rally should be less likely to create overvaluation and become a cause for broad selling. Finally, any key divergence between breadth's trend and the market averages should be taken into account because breadth changes often foreshadow turns in the averages.

Specifically, I looked for at least one pattern that spotted a simple brief upthrust in breadth after a prior rally had already carried breadth to a multiweek high. This pattern should identify the times when sellers are waiting for one more push higher to act—those who want to squeeze out the last dime of profit. As such, it may distinguish the so-called "exhaustion" peak found at the tops of many bull markets, which does not have to be related to a recent market low.

At first glance, this pattern would seem to have some similarity to the thrust buy, and it may have a few kindred qualities. A closer look will reveal key differences. A bandwagon buying spree is not a last gasp upturn in breadth.

A second sell pattern to expect is one that meets power money's known interest in selling into market strength that has developed for several days and is broad in its internal measures, but which still occurs not long after a recent breadth low. This would identify selling that would have occurred sooner, but the market had gotten an extra lift. It was overbought and underloved as the Wall Street phrase goes.

Another sell pattern to expect reflects the ability of power money to anticipate moves in the broad market averages. This is one for the technicians because it features, in their jargon, a "divergence." Divergences of all types appear in technical work and can be precursors of significant moves in the broad market. In this case, the sell pattern should appear as a divergence between breadth and one or more key market averages. Specifically, breadth should be narrowing or declining over the very short term while a broad average like the S&P 500 is still rising. Technicians or short-term traders who have a feel for the market could be expected to sell into such an internal market split.

Finally, expect a breadth pattern that appears regularly as broad market rallies run out of steam, which seems to be a common characteristic of market pauses. Here a reduction in breadth's upside momentum should occur, or a narrowing of breadth's high to low differentials may appear.

We must recognize that other types of sell patterns could exist, especially if they are more complex than those I've identified, but they await further research. Now let's explore the actual sell patterns in some detail.

# Specific Patterns

To achieve success, the sell patterns start with a precondition of a positive absolute line level through which the line must decline. I have found that 415 is the level above which no viable sell pattern has existed. No theoretical specific time frame exists for this, but since the absolute line is comprised of the 20-day maximum and minimum levels, the decline requirement is effectively limited to that period. This fixed precondition is adjusted for trading activity as was the prebuy per Part I of the Statistical Notes.

## The "Ordinary" Sell

Two of the four sell patterns are surprisingly simple. The "ordinary" one has had only five valid appearances—after 12 were rejected due to lack of two conditions. Interestingly, all valid occurrences of the ordinary sell pattern came after 1981, suggesting some relationship to the heavy institutional activity of the 1980s, possibly to program or derivative trading.

**FIGURE 2–11    July 1990 Ordinary Sell**

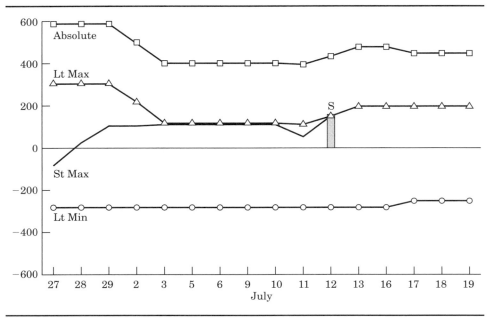

<br>

**Ordinary Sell Record**

*(12 Patterns Rejected as Invalid)*

To First Buys: 4 of 4 Profitable, 1 incomplete Ave. gain (short) 7.1%

To Five Weeks: 5 of 5 Profitable

To Three Months: 3 of 5 Profitable

To Seventh Months: 2 of 5 Profitable

The ordinary sell pattern seeks brief strength in NYSE breadth as measured by both the 20-day and 5-day maximum levels of ADS, but this occurs as something of a last gasp because it allows for only a one-day uptick to set new highs on both maximum lines. This means breadth must be near its high of the past trading month, but that high will not be set the previous day.

Specifically, SPAR asks whether the 20- and 5-day maximums are above their prior day's level and whether the prior day's levels were less than or equal to the day before that. If the answer is yes, the pattern matches the four-for-four sell–buy accuracy of the historical patterns that included the near peak of November 1983 and a market dip in December 1985. The August 1993 pattern had no buy to pair with by yearend but was not a loser (it broke even) in the fifth week after appearance. The most successful of the ordinary sell pattern's appearances occurred in July 1990 when it was within 1 percent of the all-

**FIGURE 2–12   August 1993 Ordinary Sell**

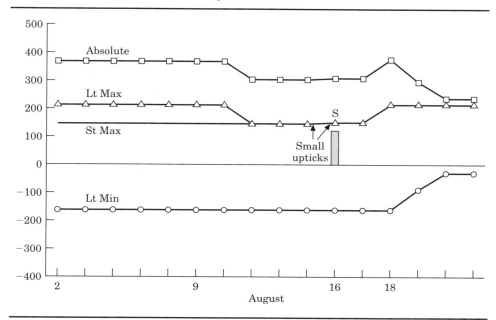

time high (see Figure 2–11). Like the other two action sells, this pattern was the subject of a revision in 1991: By adding one condition to the initial set, a dozen signals were eliminated. This also reduced the sample size from 17 to 5. Thus, this pattern must be used with some caution until a larger valid sample is developed.

## The "Short-Term Setup"

The most common action sell pattern is the "setup," which has appeared 16 times with four errors in sell–buy pairs and two incompletes. An additional 11 signals were rejected as lacking two key conditions, both related to recent levels of STMAX and LTMIN. Nevertheless, this sample size is clearly adequate for future projections. The full track record shows its short-term orientation, which allows this pattern to make the best use of SPAR's capability to foreshadow the S&P 500.

---

**Short Term Setup Sell Record**
*(11 Patterns Rejected as Invalid)*

To First Buys: 10 of 14 Profitable, 2 Incomplete Ave. gain (short) 8.3%
To Five Weeks: 12 of 16 Profitable
To Three Months: 5 of 15 Profitable, 1 Incomplete
(See Discussion and Table Below)

---

The setup pattern looks for an incipient downward movement in the five-day maximum line to below its level of five days earlier. This would signify a loss of ADS momentum, not necessarily a broad downturn. The pattern then asks whether the S&P 500 itself was rising contrarily for three consecutive days. If both these conditions are met at a level below absolute 415, the pattern matches the correct history and a sell signal is issued. In Figure 2-13, two setup sells appear near the market top in August 1987 and they show the four line ADS parameters clearly. The S&P 500 is not shown.

The success of the setup pattern is importantly qualified by a key characteristic. The market went on to higher levels relatively soon after a decline within the first month on seven of its 16 appearances. All seven were followed by a later sell pattern with no intervening buy. On all but one of those occasions, the market fell with a minimum 10 percent correction thereafter. The exception occurred in January 1993, which saw the later sell (August) but no substantial correction by January 1994. However, the October 1993 sell was also a setup type and its record is incomplete. (See 1994 Update Addendum.) However, on the eight occasions when the market did not rally meaningfully after its early dip, the market fell and produced a SPAR buy signal at lower market levels. Each of the buy signals resulted in a strong bull market, which appears to make the short-term setup sell a highly iffy signal. But, the common fact in both circumstances is that after all appearances of the setup pattern, the market declined to below its sell level within a month's time. The ensuing market action then became critical in foreshadowing both the next signal and the later market trend. The short-term setup pattern isn't iffy. It says simply (1) a market dip is

**FIGURE 2-13    August 1987 Setup Sells**

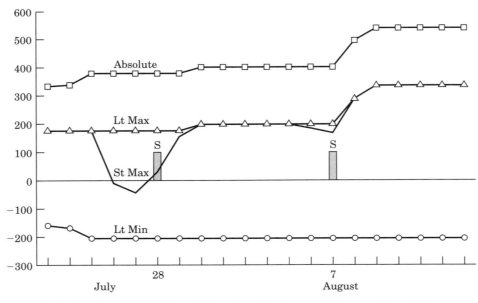

coming and 2) the subsequent market developments are to be followed. Knowing this is valuable. The rule is that if the S&P 500 follows the first market dip with a new high within 30 sessions of a setup appearance and the next correction fails to break the first dip low, expect further market gains.

Table 2–1 shows the market action following each of the setup pattern appearances since 1972.

The contrast between the two data sets is striking. The sell to sell set has consistently led to a meaningful market correction or major bear market, the sell to buy set to a new or renewed bull market. Therefore, we act on this signal in accord with these parameters.

Two periods need additional comment. In July–August 1987, the market correction began in late August, but it failed to rally to a new market high in the September rise and then fell below its first correction low. That warning came in mid-September. With the ADS picture also negative (see Chapter 6) and the Stock Model in a neutral mode, the SPAR system was giving ample warning of danger ahead.

Contrast this with January 1993, when the market rallied above its prior high after the first correction, and the second correction in late April did not break the prior correction's low. (The Stock Model was

**TABLE 2–1    Short-Term Setup Sell Appearances and Results**

KEY: The appearances are organized "Sell to Sell" and "Sell to Buy" by the type of pattern, buy or sell, that followed the setup sell. The appearance dates show the setup signal date first followed by the subsequent pattern. The Change column shows two percentages. The first is the maximum market change *between* the two patterns, and the second is the change from the first to the second pattern. The Result column indicates the market trend *after* the second pattern appeared.

Sell to Sell

| Setup/Next Dates | Change | Result |
|---|---|---|
| 9/72–10/72 | –3.5/–0.5% | Up 9%/Bear Market |
| 8/76–12/76 | –5/+0.6% | Bear Market |
| 2/77–7/77 | –6.5/–2.0% | Down 15% |
| 9/77–2/80 | –9/+22.2% | Down 13% |
| 4/85–7/85 | 0/+5.4% | 10% correction |
| 3/87–8/87 | –6.1/+9.8% | Bear Market |
| 1/93–8/93 | –.5/+4.6 | Up 5.7% / ? |

Sell to Buy

| Setup/Nex Dates | Change | Result |
|---|---|---|
| 10/72–10/74 | –43.6/–35% | Bull Market |
| 2/80–4/80 | –15.5/–11.8% | Bull Market |
| 7/85–8/85 | –3/–3.1% | Bull Market |
| 7/87–11/87 | –28/–28% | Bull Market |
| 10/88–11/88 | –4.7/+4.1% | Bull Market |
| 5/89–7/89 | –2/–0.7% | Bull Market |
| 8/91–12/91 | –4.5/–1.4% | Bull Market |
| 6/92–6/92 | 0/0% | Bull Market |
| 10/93: Incomplete: | | |

bullish.) The system's advice was no immediate trouble ahead. The October 1993 setup carried with it a march that was initially down, but then tiny dips accompanied a market rally over the next two months. Still, the S&P 500 barely reached a meaningful new high before year-end. Reading: an unenthusiastic bull continuation.

## The "Long-Term" Sell

The final true sell pattern is the complex "long-term" sell. This pattern attempts to find the rare conditions that foreshadow important market downswings during bull markets or developing bear markets. In doing so, it makes the fewest appearances—three valid occurences and four rejects—due to a revision with an additional condition in 1991. Like the waterfall buy pattern, the long-term sell pattern must be used with caution because of its small sample size.

Nevertheless, the long-term sell pattern has had success. It signaled the December 1976 market top (see Figure 2–14) within less than 2 percent in the S&P, and the June 1977 five-month high 13 percent ahead of the long slide to the March 1978 low. It also caught the March 1981 final peak within 2 percent of the November 1980 S&P high and just ahead of the Dow Jones Industrial Average's April 1981 top. Thus, all of its appearances were correct calls for the S&P 500 when tested five weeks later. Note that the long-term sell has not made an appearance since July 1985 and that was in the same presell sequence as a setup sell. (see Figure 2–15) Give it another few years.

---

**Long-Term Sell Record**

*(4 Patterns Rejected as Invalid)*

To First Buys: 3 of 3 Profitable Ave. gain (short) 4.5%

To Five Weeks: 3 of 3 Profitable

To Three Months: 3 of 3 Profitable

To Seventh Month: 3 of 3 Profitable

---

This pattern addresses all the ADS component lines plus the S&P 500 Index, and does so by seeking rises in all but the absolute line. It wants a broad rise in breadth, in other words, but not one that is moving so strongly that it is setting new highs, especially on the current day. In each of the three independent components, the long-term sell pattern looks for the current day to be above the average of the prior eight days, but for the absolute line to be below its 20-day maximum. It also imposes an additional condition that either the maximum or minimum lines be up on the pattern day, and that the S&P itself be up on action day.

At first glance, this pattern might seem to require an odd combination. What it demands is rare given the number of appearances, but it is quite common for the three basic lines to be above their recent

**FIGURE 2–14    December 1976 Long Term Sell**

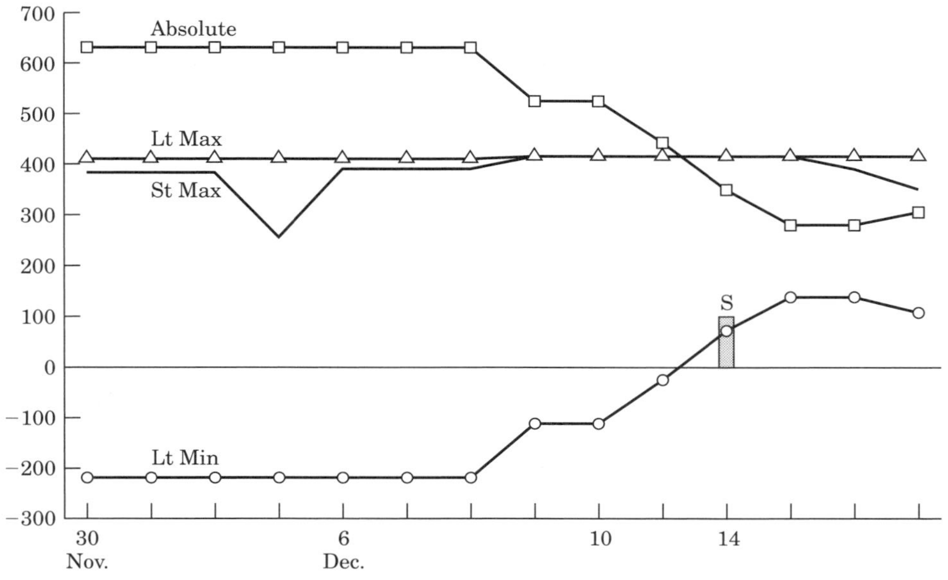

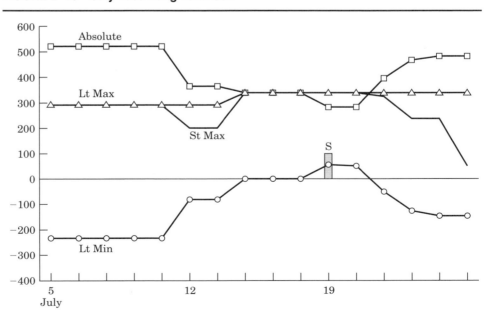

numerical averages. What is rare is to find the absolute component off its recent peak when this occurs. This means that the breadth rally has lost some of its steam due to the passage of time and, for one day at least, has done so while the S&P is on an uptick. In short, the long-term sell pattern attempts to find the power money sales that are

**FIGURE 2–15    July 1985 Long Term Sell**

occurring during the last gasp of a rally. The pattern is looking for the die-hard selling and the proverbial "exhaustion" top.

## The "Stopper"

The last pattern is named the "stopper" because of its ability to identify the ends to major market rallies. But, it is not a true action pattern because it doesn't regularly find longer term market declines following it. Fewer than half of its 26 occurrences have had succeeding down markets. Instead, the stopper's value is that the market pauses it locates are worthwhile points to stop buying or assuming a bull trend will continue. That's because not once in the stopper's appearances did the market fail to cease its rise for at least a month's time. The stopper pattern has also appeared at or close to some major and important interim tops: November–December 1972, June–July 1977, August of 1978 and 1979, March 1981, April 1982, June 1987, and January 1992.

Furthermore, while the market subsequently moved either up or down with no apparent pattern characteristic to signal it, the market's (S&P 500) meaningful turn 40 days after the pattern's end nearly always signaled the next meaningful trend. Even the June 1987 appearance caught a market pause and the last upswing of 8 percent before it was neatly terminated by SPAR setup sells in late July and early August.

The stopper pattern is easy to spot on a graph of the four ADS components. See Figure 2-16. It first requires that the minimum line move into positive territory. This is fairly rare, but it will automatically bring the absolute line down as LTMIN is subtracted from LTMAX: a posi-

**FIGURE 2–16    August 1993 Stopper**

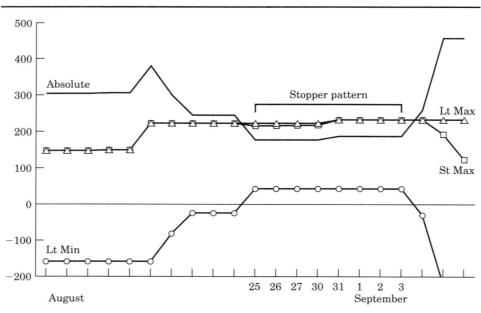

tive number subtracted from another positive. When the LTMIN line positive movement coincides with the LTMAX line *above* the absolute line, the stopper pattern is generated.

To determine the next market trend, we note the S&P high and low during the pattern. The range will not be great. Since 1980 it has not exceeded 6 percent. The market's next meaningful trend will be in the direction of the S&P's move above that high or below that low during the following eight trading weeks. Any S&P move greater than 2 percent outside the high–low range qualifies. Table 2–2 shows the accuracy of these rules; only January 1979 and June 1989 were exceptions. This sort of record tempts one to consider the stopper pattern as fully valid as the other sells. However, the subsequent market breakouts varied widely in occurrence, from one month to two months, a condition that makes this pattern far looser than any other. Until further research produces a tighter set of conditions, consider the stopper to be just that and expect the subsequent S&P break or a new SPAR pattern arrival to be the action point.

New SPAR patterns often appear following stoppers, which makes the subsequent market call simple. Twelve of the 26 stopper appearances saw a SPAR signal within 20 trading days of the stopper's end. Six of those appearances were buys, another reminder that a market pause does not necessarily lead to a downturn. In addition, following

**TABLE 2–2  Stopper Pattern Results**

| Pattern | S&P Hi/Lo | Break During Next 40 Sessions | Subseq. Action |
|---|---|---|---|
| 11/17–12/12/72 | 115–19 | Down | New bear market |
| 1/24–2/12/75 | 76–82 | Up | Continued bull market |
| 1/21–2/24/76 | 99–102 | No break | Rally to 9/76 top |
| 7/8–7/16/76 | 103–105 | No break | Flat to 9/76 top |
| 6/30–7/5/77 | 100 | Down | Continued bear market |
| 8/7–8/18/78 | 103–105 | Down | Continued bear market |
| 1/29–1/30/79 | 101 | Down | Rally to 10/79 hi |
| 8/21–8/23/79 | 108 | Down | Continued bear market |
| 3/24–3/27/81 | 134–37 | Down | Continued bear market |
| 4/15–4/28/82 | 115–19 | Down | Continued bear market |
| 5/4–5/13/83 | 164–66 | Up | Up to June high, correction, bull market |
| 8/27–8/31/84 | 166–67 | No break | Flat to 12/84 |
| 2/1–2/20/85 | 179–83 | No break | Flat to 5/85 |
| 6/4–6/10/85 | 189–90 | Down | Interim top 7/85, then bull market |
| 11/25–12/20/85 | 200–212 | Up | Continued bull market |
| 2/21–3/25/86 | 224–36 | Up | Continued bull market |
| 6/22–6/25/87 | 306–309 | Up | Bull market to 8/87 |
| 3/8–3/9/88 | 267–69 | Down | Ranging to 10/88 |
| 1/24–2/7/89 | 285–99 | No break | Flat to late April, bull market |
| 6/11–6/12/89 | 326 | Down | Continued bull market late July |
| 2/14–2/23/91 | 364–69 | Up | Continued bull market |
| 1/20/92 | 416 | Down | Lows 4/92, 7/92 |
| 11/9–11/16-92 | 418–23 | Up | Continued bull market |
| 2/5–2/11/93 | 445–49 | Up | Low 4/93, bull market |
| 8/25–9/3/93 | 460–63 | Up | Continued bull market |
| 1/19–1/22/94 | 474–75 | Down | |

the stopper only two of those 12 SPAR signals went in the opposite direction to the S&P trend. The sell on December 13, 1985, came within the stopper pattern of November 25–December 20. Thereafter the market modestly declined and rallied, but that SPAR signal was quickly reversed with a buy on January 13, 1986. The S&P call proved to be the correct one.

The other was the SPAR sell on July 29, 1987, when both the S&P trend and the SPAR sells were proved correct. Therefore, the rule to follow the S&P trend after the stopper pattern holds, but one must be alert to a possible SPAR action pattern that reverses it.

The SPAR patterns that followed stoppers were:

| | |
|---|---|
| Buy February 26, 1975 | Buy June 2, 1983 |
| Buy March 16, 1976 | Sell December 13, 1985 |
| Sell August 16, 1976 | Sell July 29, 1987 |
| Sell June 30, 1977 | Buy February 27, 1989 |
| Sell March 25, 1981 | Buy July 3, 1989 |
| Sell April 23, 1982 | Buy December 16, 1991 |

The stopper is a useful pattern to identify as a time for a halt in the action. It must not be read as a medium-term market forecast, however, because the market's resolution of the pause is the important trend to follow.

In conclusion, the SPAR patterns are highly rigorous in their conditions for appearance and, in aggregate, have strong probabilities against occurring at random. Their appearances have the lowest statistical category of randomness, whether they are measured buy–sell and sell–buy or for fixed periods.

Perhaps SPAR's greatest flaw is its inability to announce the time frame for which a signal is to apply. The signals can reverse direction after two or three months, although that's not common. This occurred within six months after a signal only about one-quarter of the time. And, not one of the reversals lost money in the S&P. I'll deal at greater length with reversals when discussing specific strategies, but for now recall that this "flaw" produced more than four times the return of the S&P buy-hold by trading the S&P cash index with a 94 percent accuracy rate for two decades. We also know that SPAR signals are most reliable in the month following issuance and again after six months. In between, the market often runs counter to them temporarily. Thus, it is sensible with this record is to not attempt to forecast the intermediate market trend with SPAR signals, but to act on all their appearances. See the 1994 Update.

We are now ready to complete the discussion of the primary use of the SPAR system with the addition of the Stock Model of outside indicators, which is used to determine how aggressively to act on each SPAR signal.

**Author's Use Tip**

The key aspect to understand about SPAR is that it is a positioning measure, not a market timer. Think of the SPAR signals as safe harbors to sail into while the market flood swirls by. Keeping a solid anchoring in power money's beliefs about market direction is a critical advantage to have in this era of instant, pervasive, and contradictory market opinions. The trick is to realize you must let go of a belief when power money does. It's simple to see—a new SPAR signal. Mental flexibility is the quality that allows that release to occur and permits spotting the new harbor for the next tide. Just remember that SPAR has never said "let go" and been wrong.

# 3 Module Two: Quantification

Addressing the matter of how strongly to act upon SPAR's signals is no small issue and few investment systems deal with this subject. Normally, market timing approaches offer their signals and assume the degree of action will always be the same. The idea is that a sell is a sell. This is a critical flaw in most timing methods. The market is too dynamic to be acted upon with uniformity at all buy and sell directives from any system. As a result, "errors" are created and the concept of timing takes a bad rap for lack of *quantification*. If there is no discipline on this point, signal success alone will often produce only mediocre profits.

In creating the SPAR strategy, as opposed to discovering the SPAR patterns, I've attempted to address this omission. The 1991–93 period provides cases in point. SPAR patterns issued signals as follows. (My advice caused action a few points higher at each of the last three signals.)

Buy: January 17, 1991, at S&P 328

Sell: August 16, 1991, at S&P 389.9

Buy: December 16, 1991, at S&P 384.4

Sell: June 15, 1992, at S&P 410.1

Buy: June 30, 1992, at S&P 408.1

Sell: January 13, 1993, at S&P 433

Sell: August 16, 1993, at S&P 453.4

Sell: October 28, 1993, at S&P 467.7

With the advantage of hindsight, how aggressively should these signals have been acted upon? The market soared at or just after both the 1991 buys, but dropped only briefly and worked higher after that year's sell. Thus, the July and December buys should have been taken aggressively and the August sell mildly, even though the latter preceded the Soviet coup market collapse by only two trading days.

In 1992, the market again moved higher soon after the June sell and buy, so the sell should have been mild and the buy aggressive. In 1993, the January sell should have been mild, despite the 82 point Dow Jones Industrial Average (DJIA) smash 30 days later, as the market was higher both before and after that hit. On the basis of market action in the ensuing four months, the August 1993 sell action also should have been mild as the market dipped briefly, but new highs were set in October. The October sell should have been taken moderately as the S&P dropped immediately and was below the sell level at year-end, even though a minor new high was reached in the interim and in January 1994.

The question is, how does one determine the correct level of aggressiveness? Only two outside indicators provide an answer for each situation. They are the short-term interest rate trend and the market's own momentum, two measures I've worked with for some 15 years with fine results in determining market moods. Combined, the two measures form a Stock Model and are collectively referred to as such. During 1991–93, interest rates and market momentum were both positive (bullish) at each of the eight signals, suggesting a simple rule that would have placed an investor in the correct action mode in all eight.

The rule says (1) act aggressively when *both Model indicators conform* to the direction of the SPAR signal; for example, buy strongly when both are bullish, sell strongly when both are bearish; (2) act mildly when both indicators are *opposite* to the signal, for example, a sell signal with a bullish indicator pair; and (3) act moderately when the indicators are *mixed*, (4) act *moderately* on all *second* or greater consecutive sells under bullish model conditions.

Using my specific measures for the short-term interest rate trend and market momentum, both indicators were bullish from November 12, 1990, when lagging momentum turned positive. According to the rule, the January 1991 buy should have been aggressive, as subsequent market action proved correct. With double bullish readings for all remaining signals, the August 1991 sell was correctly taken mildly, while the buy in December at a lower market level was taken aggressively. The higher level sell in June 1992 was mild while the two week later buy was taken aggressively.

The January 1993 sell was at a nicely higher level, but like that of August 1991, came opposite the bullish indicator pair, so was taken mildly. The same occurred in August 1993, but it was a second consecutive sell so it was taken moderately, not mildly. The market measured by the DJIA lost 115 points in September 1993 before marching on to new highs. (The S&P dipped 2 percent.) The October sell was also taken moderately because no sell could be taken aggressively under bullish Stock Model conditions or it would virtually obviate the model reading. Note that the market immediately fell more than 2 percent and was below the signal level at year-end.

In sum, the concept worked during 1991–93, but the period was not marked by isolated cases of quantitative success. This two-part discipline would have worked splendidly throughout the full 22 years of SPAR study, as Table 3-1 shows.

Model changes are shown with the indicator causing the change in parenthesis. SPAR signals show S&P closing levels at which they occurred.

**TABLE 3-1    SPAR Signal Quantification**

### 1972

| | |
|---|---|
| January: | Model bullish (MA) |
| May 12 | Buy aggressive at S&P 106.4 |
| August: | Model down to neutral (STIR) |
| September 1 | Sell moderate at 111.5 |
| October 10 | Sell aggressive at 110 |

(Year-end 118.1, subsequent high January 1973 at 120)

### 1973

| | |
|---|---|
| March: | Model down to bearish (MA) |

(Year-end 97.6, subsequent low October 1974 at 61)

### 1974

| | |
|---|---|
| October 7 | Buy mild at 65 |
| October 17 | Buy moderate at 71.2 |
| end October: | Model up to Neutral (STIR) |
| December 10 | Buy aggressive at 67.3 |

(Year-end 68.6)

### 1975

| | |
|---|---|
| Mid-February: | Model up to bullish (MA) |
| February 26 | Buy aggressive at 80.4 |
| April 10 | Buy aggressive at 83.8 |
| July 30 | Buy aggressive at 88.8 |
| Dec. 4 | Buy aggressive at 87.8 |
| Dec. 11 | Buy aggressive at 87.8 |

(year-end 90.2)

### 1976

| | |
|---|---|
| March 16 | Buy aggressive at 100.9 |
| Aug. 16 | Sell mild at 104.4 |
| early Oct.: | Model down to neutral (MA) |
| Dec. 14 | Sell moderate at 105.1 |

(Year-end and subsequent high 107.5)

### 1977

| | |
|---|---|
| February 1 | Sell aggressive at 102.5 |
| late April: | Model down to bearish (STIR) |
| June 30 | Sell aggressive at 100.5 |
| Sept. 15 | Sell aggressive at 95.2 |

(Year-end 95.1, subsequent low March 1978 at 87.3)

### 1978

| | |
|---|---|
| late April: | Model up to neutral (MA) |
| late October: | Model down to bearish (MA) |

(year-end 96.1)

### 1979

| | |
|---|---|
| Late March: | Model up to neutral (MA) |
| Mid-October: | Model down to bearish (MA) |

(year-end 107.9)

### 1980

| | |
|---|---|
| Mid-January: | Model up to neutral (MA) |
| February 7 | Sell moderate at 116.3 |
| Early March: | Model down to bearish (MA) |
| April 15 | Buy mild at 102.6 |
| May: | Model up to bullish (both MA and STIR) |
| August 29 | Buy aggressive at 122.4 |
| End Nov.: | Model down to neutral (STIR) |

(High November @ 140, year-end 135.3)

**TABLE 3–1**   *continued*

### 1981

| | |
|---|---|
| March 25 | Sell moderate at 137.1 |
| Mid-July: | Model down to bearish (MA) |
| October 14 | Buy mild at 118.8 |
| End October: | Model up to neutral (STIR) |
| | (year-end 122.6) |

### 1982

| | |
|---|---|
| January 28 | Buy moderate at 118.9 |
| April 23 | Sell moderate at 118.6 |
| August 13 | Buy moderate at 103.9 |
| August 16 | Buy aggressive at 104.1 |
| August 23: | Model up to bullish (MA) |
| | (year-end 140.6) |

### 1983

| | |
|---|---|
| June 2 | Buy aggressive at 162.6 |
| End June: | Model down to neutral (STIR) |
| November 11 | Sell moderate at 164.4 |
| | (year-end 164.9) |

### 1984

| | |
|---|---|
| February 6: | Model down to bearish (MA) |
| August 1 | Buy mild at 154.1 |
| Early Aug. | Model up to neutral (MA) |
| End October: | Model up to bullish |
| | (year-end 167.2) |

### 1985

| | |
|---|---|
| April 25 | Sell mild at 183.4 |
| July 12 | Sell moderate at 193.3 |
| August 8 | Buy aggressive at 189 |
| December 13 | Sell mild at 209.9 |
| | (year-end 206.9) |

### 1986

| | |
|---|---|
| January 13 | Buy aggressive at 206.7 |
| April 8 | Buy aggressive at 233.5 |
| | (year-end 242.2) |

### 1987

| | |
|---|---|
| March 19 | Sell mild at 294.1 |
| mid-April: | Model down to neutral (STIR) |
| July 29 | Sell moderate at 315.7 |
| August 7 | Sell moderate at 323 (same seq.) |
| October 15 | Model down to bearish (MA) |
| November 30 | Buy mild at 230.2 |
| December 21 | Model up to neutral (MA) |
| | (year-end 247.1) |

### 1988

| | |
|---|---|
| January 15 | Buy moderate at 252 |
| October 17 | Sell moderate at 276.4 |
| November 30 | Buy moderate at 273.7 |
| | (year-end 277.6) |

### 1989

| | |
|---|---|
| February 27 | Buy moderate at 287.8 |
| May 26 | Sell moderate at 321.6 |
| July 3 | Buy moderate at 319.2 |
| August 4: | Model up to bullish (STIR) |
| October 31 | Buy aggressive at 340.3 |
| December 20 | Buy aggressive at 342.8 |
| | (year-end 353.4) |

*continued*

**TABLE 3–1**    *concluded*

### 1990

| | |
|---|---|
| January 23: | Model down to neutral (MA) |
| March 12: | Model up to bullish (MA) |
| May 4 | Buy aggressive at 338.4 |
| July 12 | Sell mild at 365.4 |
| August 6 | Model down to neutral (MA) |
| October 1 | Buy moderate at 314.9 |
| IN REAL TIME | |
| October 26 | Buy aggressive at 304.7 |
| November 12 | Model up to bullish |

(year-end 330.2)

### 1991

| | |
|---|---|
| January 17 | Buy aggressive at 328 |
| August 14 | Sell mild at 389.9 |
| December 16 | Buy aggressive at 384.5 |

(year-end 417.1)

### 1992

| | |
|---|---|
| June 15 | Sell mild at 410.1 |
| June 30 | Buy aggressive at 408.1 |
| October 6 | Model down to neutral (MA) |
| October 27 | Model up to bullish (MA) |

(year-end 435.7)

### 1993

| | |
|---|---|
| January 13 | Sell mild at 433 |
| August 16 | Sell moderate at 453 |
| October 29 | Sell moderate at 467.8 |

(year-end 465.5)

# Origins

The indicators have a great deal of theoretical and practical work to commend them. I initially addressed them in my 1990 book, *There's Always A Bull Market*, as part of the discussion of the Stock Model for determining bull market conditions. The interest rate trend indicator has been taken wholly intact from that incarnation and needs only a brief background discussion.

From the capital asset pricing model, we know that stock *values* can be determined by the formula:

$$P = D \div (k-g)$$

where:

$D$ = the dividend amount

$P$ = the present value of an infinite stream of dividend income, $g$ = the annual growth rate of dividend income, $k$ = a discount rate for that income in the market *g* is determined by analyst estimates for dividend growth potential of a given stock or index. *K* is calculated from the differential of the historical return of stocks to bonds times the current U.S. Treasury long-term bond rate times the given stock's beta.

($k$ = LBR × (SR/BR) × beta.

Substitution in the formula verifies that increases in the denominator from rising (1) long-term bond rates, (LBR) (2) the differential in bond (BR) to stock (SR) return, and (3) a stock's beta will cause the present value of the dividend return to decline as surely as a decline in the dividend itself. Federal Reserve efforts to drive short term interest rates higher through the linkage of short-term and long-term government rates also will cause the present value of the dividend to decline.

Measuring Federal Reserve intent to move short-term rates is relatively easy to do in the money market, while estimating *valid* changes in bond and stock return differentials is more difficult. It follows that one fast way to estimate a change in stock values is through the use of an interest rate indicator that reflects the Fed's influence on short-term rates, an influence that is crucial. Any effort to fight that bias is counterproductive of stock profits, as many investors have learned through sad experience.

The measure I use is STIR—short-term interest rate index—but any smoothed measure of short-term interest rates that incorporates the Federal Reserve's intent will do.

STIR is calculated by averaging the weekly 90-day T-bill coupon equivalent yield with the weekly average federal funds rate and multiplying the result by the Federal Reserve Board (FRB) discount rate. Movements of STIR above and below its 33- and 45-week moving averages (MA's) call the rate trends. During fast-moving rate changes, the 33-week MA is the trigger, otherwise it's the 45-week measure.

I have used a 39-week or 200-day moving average of either the DJIA or the S&P 500 as the market momentum indicator for most of the 15 years I've published an advisory service. This MA's role is to ensure a tempering of action on SPAR signals when the "market" is moving contrarily to both SPAR and FRB intent. That is rare and, importantly, usually lasts only a short time. Of course, the 39 week and 200 day MAs are widely followed market trend indicators and are thus faulted with popularity.

Probably the two most significant problems with these MA's are their tendencies to whipsaw in trading range markets like those of 1978–80 and their tardiness in great rushes like those in August 1982, February and August 1984, and January 1991. The worst example occurred in October 1987 when the MA produced a sale midsession on the Thursday before Black Monday, 16 percent below the August 1987 high.

I could accept tardiness when it's only one of three action determinants and an *aggressiveness* measure, not a timing one. For example, recall that in 1987 SPAR signaled sells in late July and early August. Also, in the spring the Fed began raising interest rates sufficiently to trip our STIR index in mid-April. That Fed intent continued until the October crash. Despite the lateness of the market MA to perform, followers of my approach would theoretically have been well prepared with *moderate* sells in July–August 1987 as a result of the down-ticked Stock Model reading and the SPAR signals.

However, accepting this doesn't address the indicator flaw. A sound discipline demands refinements. One modification to the MA deals with both its potential surge tardiness and its trading range whipsaws: a rate of change filter.

In *There's Always a Bull Market*, I recommended use of a 2 percent fixed filter band on either side of the moving average as a trigger point rather than the MA itself. This has subsequently proved valid, if not totally errorproof. Better are the Bollinger bands,[1] which tighten the filter when the market is relatively flat and widen it when major changes have occurred. The theory behind the Bollinger bands is that when the market is ranging in a relatively narrow band, it will periodically trade very close to a valid MA, but will do so without conviction. Moves toward the MA will be measured, not rushed. However, when a trend out of the band begins, investors wish to spot it quickly. A narrowed filter range during the trading range does that. On the other hand, when the market is clearly trending, by definition it is moving with conviction. At this time, it should be given room to move without tight limits on corrections. A variable filter should also accomplish this.

The variable filter can do something else. Trending periods often cause the market to move well away from a standard MA with a fixed filter, causing the MA to be overtaken late in a trend change. This was the problem in October 1987 when the MA was far below the market, while the reverse occurred during August 1982 and August 1984 when the MA was well above the leading averages. Clearly, this is a conundrum.

Handily, market trend changes have one other characteristic that affords a solution. They almost never reverse quickly from a strong trend in one direction to a strong move in the other. Even the seemingly abrupt turn in July 1990 saw the S&P in a trading range of 15 points, about 4 percent, for eight weeks before the break. A properly adaptable MA filter would have narrowed for the last two weeks and caught the downswing within another five points.

The Bollinger bands address both moving average weaknesses because they utilize a measure of standard deviation of the subject index or stock to adjust their width. Most computerized trading programs now contain calculations for these bands. My use of the bands produced no important whipsaws in the test period from early 1984 through 1993, and the bands caught all major market trends within about 10 percent of their initiation. One minor whipsaw, that of October 6, 1992, took place when the lower band was validly broken within two days of the actual S&P low. That was, however, the only such occurrence in 11 years, and it was reversed within two weeks at less than a 3 percent disadvantage. In all, the bands have done an adequate

---

[1]Bollinger Capital Management, Manhattan Beach, CA 90266

job of advising when to become aggressive on SPAR signals, especially when coupled with the STIR index.

# Systematizing

Transforming the rule for our two-indicator Stock Model into practice is accomplished by first noting the three modes the rule creates for the Stock Model: bullish, neutral, and bearish. Two positive indicator readings are bullish, two negative readings are bearish, and a mixed reading is neutral. As noted, each SPAR signal is then acted upon by the degree to which Stock Model readings align with or contradict the signal. SPAR buys in bullish periods are aggressive, but in bearish periods they are mild, and vice versa for sells. Most important, the model can never change the SPAR signal; it can only modify the aggressiveness with which one acts.

One further factor can be taken into account in our quantification thinking: multiple SPAR signals in the same direction. This has been SPAR's historic means of telling us when power money is adding to its positions in or out of the market, the effect of which is to increase the Stock Model's aggressiveness reading by one level until the maximum is reached. Second mild sells become moderate, not mild, and so forth. However, this requires an adjustment to our model rule since three consecutive SPAR signals *opposite* to the Stock Model reading would virtually negate the latter. Therefore, the maximum opposite weighting is moderate, not aggressive.

# Analysis

Even a casual review of the track record (Table 3–1) shows that the Stock Model and SPAR signals work hand in glove. On no occasion throughout the 22 years was an investor wrongly positioned for any major trend. Because this record is important in assessing the capability of SPAR signals and Stock Model interaction, it is analyzed below.

**1.** At the end of the "nifty fifty" era in stocks in 1972, a moderate sell in September and an aggressive sell in October would have positioned investors well for the 1973–74 bear market start three months later. SPAR then stayed out of the bear's subsequent 21-month mauling.

**2.** During the two-month beginning of the next great bull market in the fall of 1974, investors would have been well invested through three consecutive buy patterns: mild, moderate, and aggressive. As the market roared higher, six more aggressive buys followed into early 1976.

**3.** Three consecutive sells—mild, moderate, and aggressive— would have left investors in heavily defensive positions at the top on December 31, 1976, and carried that posture through the ranging bear market of 1978–79. (See the "Criticism" section following.)

**4.** A mild buy caught the bear market lows of early 1980 and was followed by a moderate buy in August. SPAR's August buy was late in this brief bull market, but still caught the 15 percent runup to the November peak.

**5.** The 1981–82 bear market was traded with a pair of early buys— mild and a moderate—to a moderate sell in April 1982 at the trading top prior to the decline to the summer lows. The trades were about breakeven in terms of the S&P 500.

**6.** The major bull market starting in August 1982 would have been caught with a moderate buy and an aggressive buy within 2 percent of the exact low. These buys were followed by a tardy, but slightly profitable, aggressive buy in June 1983.

**7.** The decent (15 percent) six-month correction of 1984 would have been tipped off by a single moderate sell in November 1983.

**8.** The bull market resumption would have been tagged by the mild buy of August 1984. The Stock Model's shift to neutral on the August market surge and to bullish on interest rate movements in October clearly indicated the power potential of this market period.

**9.** Trading in 1985 was marked by two successively higher sells in April and July, an aggressive buy in August which was a bit above the correction lows of September, and a mild sell in December. All were profitable. (See also the "Criticism" section.)

**10.** Aggressive buys in January and April 1986 would have set up excellent profits by the mild March 1987 precorrection sell. A pair of moderate sells in July and early August came at an average of just 5 percent below the S&P high.

**11.** The post-crash lows would have been well addressed by a mild buy in November 1987 and a moderate buy in January 1988, then traded at a moderate sell in October 1988 and a quick post-correction rebuy in November just in time for the 1989 bull run.

**12.** Investors would have taken profits once during 1989 from a moderate sell in May, but would have rebought moderately in July and become aggressive in October and December and again in May 1990. (See "Criticism" section.)

**13.** The isolated mild sell in July 1990 was better at timing than aggressiveness, but in fairness the bear dive was over only three months later.

**14.** The moderate and aggressive buys at the lows in October 1990 rivaled similar buys in 1974 in accuracy and strength and would have positioned investors very well for the following bull market. Taking corrections into account, more buys occurred until 1993 with the exception of one mild sell before the failed Soviet coup in August 1991 and another of record brevity in June 1992.

**15.** The long, slow top formation of 1993 was treated to a mild sell in January and a pair of moderate sells in August and October. These averaged an S&P level of 454 (with the sale refinements I advised at the time), which was only 2.8 percent below the 1993 year-end S&P mark and well within SPAR's normal "noise" level of 5 to 6 percent.

In sum, this interactive record of one market phenomenon and two independent market indicators is unusual, especially considering its simplicity.

# Criticism

The record is not without flaws. Most of these are short term in nature, with the exception of the first. The lack of any SPAR signals during 1978–79 reflects the strongly defensive mode of SPAR and the model during the period 1976–77, and rightly so. But the 1978–79 time frame could sensibly have been traded on a short- to medium-term basis. SPAR's refusal to do so when the Stock Model was also bearish gives a clue to SPAR's overall attitude and is explained by how institutions act. All other things being equal, when institutions perceive only a mediocre (or unfavorable) upside potential, as a group they pass up the opportunity to buy. In aggregate, they do not "trade" the market. Nevertheless, the system can be faulted for not picking at least one good buy point near the 1978 or 1979 lows.

The fast-changing market of 1980 was also interesting. The Stock Model's uptick to neutral in January prevented the February SPAR setup sell from becoming aggressive, but that type of sell forecasts only a correction within a month's trading time, and one followed with perfect timing. It was unusually steep, though, and was prompted by the Fed's sudden decision to change credit card rules, which power money did not anticipate.

The model's break to bearish in late March then seemed ill-timed, but the market was falling rapidly. The timing of the next buy on April 15 was impeccable in hindsight, coming within 4 percent of the exact S&P low.

The model then played catch-up in May, upticking twice to a bullish reading that foreshadowed the splendid market run to the November high, with another SPAR buy in August to boot. The model's backdown in November caught that high mark nicely and it allowed the March 1981 SPAR sell to be moderate, not mild, which also was excellent in strength and timing. The sell came only three S&P points below the actual November 1980 high and preceded a bear run of almost 20 percent. In sum, the 1980–81 SPAR–Stock Model interaction could be faulted only on very short- run results, but it finished the day profitably and correctly positioned.

SPAR's out–in trading during 1985 appears to have been unnecessary even though it produced profits each time. In reality, of course, there is nothing wrong with taking profits except for their impact on taxable accounts. Institutions, of course, are tax- advantaged. Moreover, the Stock Model's bullishness kept sales from being aggressive but allowed the buys to be so, clearly a plus for the SPAR–Stock Model interaction.

The 1989–90 SPAR foible was that the October and December 1989 buys were early in light of the January 1990 correction. The fact that they were aggressive buys did not help. Nevertheless, the correction from the average late 1989 buy levels was less than 6 percent, close to SPAR's normal noise range, and the buys were profitable by about 7 percent at the July 1990 sell. In 1990, power money had an uncomfortable January through March but "smiled all the way to the bank" from July through year-end.

The year 1993 deserves comment because of its apparently early sell signals. In this sense, they are a repeat of spring and early summer 1985 although no buy signal came along to reverse the picture. The year 1993 gave investors little reason to become strongly bullish or bearish. High market valuations and rising long-term interest rates in the last four months largely offset the positive news of rising corporate profits. The S&P 500 finished the year with only a 7 percent gain. Against this, the split readings of SPAR sells versus a bullish Stock Model aptly reflected the market's background. Clients were advised in November 1993, "we know that trouble is coming or that SPAR will reverse course [to a buy.] Our reduced stock positions have us prepared for a problem, but there is little reason to yet become aggressive sellers or to expect an imminent major decline." We went into 1994 with a fully appropriate position: moderately underinvested and mildly bullish. (See also the 1994 Update.)

The year 1993 was also noted for SPAR's consistent sell signals to pinpoint short term market corrections, which were expected to be mild or moderate. The January and October signals were short-term setups, a type that forecasts corrections within a month of its appearance. The fast 1 percent and 2 percent dips of February and November came right on schedule, and the ordinary sell of August was feted with a deterioration of almost 4 percent in the Dow Jones Industrials in September. Because the market made only modest gains for the full year, the SPAR–Stock Model advice for corrections that equalled nearly the full rise in the S&P 500 was no minor accomplishment.

## Interaction Rules

The record again makes it clear that SPAR and the Stock Model get things remarkably right, even with modest peccadillos. Accordingly, I've found that the proper way to deal with the interaction of these two systems is to view them like putting the pieces of a puzzle together. The more pieces that fall in place in one direction, the more likely the market will take that direction. Sometimes we get only one or two pieces such as the single sell of July 1990 in bullish Stock Model conditions. Sometimes we get many pieces, such as the 10 straight buys and the model switch from bearish to bullish from October 1974 to March

1976. A large number of pieces are not necessary for a significant market change (e.g., July 1990), but they do increase the probability that a change will occur.

Should one also expect to act every time the Stock Model changes? So far I've assumed one should not, but the idea has merit as I recommended before I discovered the SPAR patterns. Looking at the 31 Stock Model changes since 1971, we see that only eight of them made outright poor market calls: two each in 1978 and 1979, and one each in 1980, 1981, 1990, and 1992. All but one of those, October 1981, came from MA switches, not from STIR. The obvious implication is that MA changes are less reliable than interest rates as market trend forecasters. Note, also that six of those eight changes came from the period 1978–81 when the fixed filter variety of MA was used. I've already dismissed it as too loose. The revised MA for 1982–93 recorded nine successful calls in 11 tries, which suggests this MA is less faulty. Still, several were fairly late, so MA crossovers are a weak link in deciding upon additional action from the model alone.

My bottom-line recommendation is to go with the strongest theory-practice combination, which is to *consider* taking further action only when Stock Model changes arise from changes in *interest rate* trends. Do so then only if one or more SPAR signals has not already brought your market positions to comfortable levels *in line* with the direction of the model change. This keeps moving average changes in a tempering role for SPAR signal aggressiveness.

To be sure, certain investors may find this takes some getting used to. Institutional professionals who are free to increase and decrease stock positions as they see fit should have no problem in overlaying these aspects of SPAR system onto their present strategies. This part of the system is tracking what the aggregate of their peers is doing—that's a reality check at a minimum. The model's independent cross-check on signals through its control of aggressiveness provides the system with built-in safeguards. Thus combined, this segment of the system should be able to place professionals on the right side of major market trends nearly all the time.

Serious individual investors, especially those with mind-sets toward a trading approach, will find they need to become more attuned to institutional thinking. This means adaptation, but not to a belief that institutions are always right—because they aren't—nor to an alignment with institutional gunslingers who don't fit the aggregate actions that SPAR reveals. Rather, the SPAR system requires adaptation to institutional longer-range thinking but with a willingness to take short-term steps as necessary. Specifically, all investors should keep the following primary considerations in mind when dealing with SPAR–Stock Model interaction.

**1.** Expect to make sales at a modest level below a major market top. Consider all mild and moderate sells to be profit taking on a scale-up basis. Remember, SPAR reveals sell *patterns*, not top-of-the-market identifications even though it's quite good at the latter. Moreover, the more sells one makes at higher prices, the closer to the actual top one must be. On *average*, SPAR caught all major tops within 3.6 percent for two decades, not on first sales in sequence.

**2.** Don't expect that signaled patterns are set in concrete. Nothing lasts forever. Power money doesn't mind buying one month and selling the next, and it often does both at the same time. Note that SPAR has never created a double reversal—for example buy, sell, buy—within a few months. When SPAR reverses itself once, it gets on the right side. You should be flexible enough to change direction when it does. (See also 1994 Update.)

**3.** The Stock Model's cross-check capability is powerful because it offers two *independent* and proven controls over the degree of action. However, the quantitative indicators of interest rates and market momentum cannot overrule the direction of SPAR signals.

**4.** SPAR appears to expect a noise level for market moves below which it won't generate a pattern. Historically, that has been 5 percent to 6 percent in the S&P. If that's the extent of a move that power money anticipates, not enough trades will be generated to show up as a pattern. If you expect an error factor in this percentage range, you'll be more attuned to SPAR signals. Of course, some sell signals appear to have called for trades in the 5 percent to 6 percent range. The signals from 1991 through 1993 are good examples because they led to small market declines in the short term. Almost all SPAR sell signals have led to modest short-term declines. Using six weeks from the signal date as an arbitrary cutoff, the S&P 500 declines within that period for all 24 sell signals averaged only 3.6 percent. No matter whether the SPAR signals are categorized, mild, moderate, or aggressive, or whether the Stock Model readings are bullish, neutral, or bearish, the *average* correction per category is still 3 percent to 4 percent within six weeks. Those numbers are indeed modest, but they mask a wide range: −1 percent to −16 percent.

The implications of the numbers are also important. First, the Stock Model does not do a good job of differentiating between the types of SPAR sell signals in the short term. Second, do not expect notable market reactions immediately after any sell signal, especially under bullish or neutral model readings. Third, the cumulative number of signals in one direction is more important than the model's degree of aggressiveness for any one signal. Fourth, the signals are still worthwhile to act upon because only three of the 24 trackable sell signals produced less than a 1 percent short-term decline. Moreover, some market reactions have become strong very quickly (three from 7 percent to 16 percent), while others have led to major bear markets within two to three months rather than an arbitrary six weeks.

The four numbered primary considerations and the four implications form the interpretative rules for interaction of the Stock Model with SPAR signals. They are worth remembering. It is also important to understand that SPAR can be used independently from the stock model, but if so, investors will do well to substitute other outside market indicators to quantify SPAR actions.

We can now add another element to our market positioning discourse, the use of futures and options for hedging or trading within the SPAR system.

---

**Author's Use Tip**

Use the Stock Model only to modify the degree of action to take on SPAR's signals. Don't make the mistake of thinking it is sometimes contradictory. Probably the best example of the Stock Model's aid to SPAR came in 1993 when the model remained bullish—saying there was little market risk—while SPAR gave three sell signals into higher market levels. At first glance, this seemed contradictory. It wasn't. It was just power money unloading stocks as the market became higher valued. Power money recognized all along the point which many investors missed: There was little immediate downside to worry about.

# 4 Futures and Options Potential

## The Dramatic Futures Record

An appropriate question to raise next is how do SPAR and the Stock Model fare in the high-risk futures and options markets if they have the capability to generate substantial profits in the cash markets? The answer carries some caveats. Let's begin by reviewing the futures record, which takes into account both long and short trades (see Table 4–1).

## Analysis

Of a total of 35 buy–sell and sell–buy trades from 1982 (the start of S&P 500 futures trading) through 1993, 32 were completed. Shown in the right-hand column of Table 4–1, they generated a net gain of 1080.95 S&P 500 futures points, with only one loss of 4.90 (from April 25 to August 8, 1985.) That's a 33.78 point net average gain per contract, or about 80 percent profit on the initial margin on each trade—a record that's hard to beat. However, the average holding period was more than nine months, a time frame that seems like eternity in the world of futures trading. That raises the question of drawdowns a trader had to stand. (Drawdowns are losses in cash deposits made to secure futures trades.) These are shown in the first 20 session column after the signal by a minus at the high or low dates. Note, only nine of 36 finished this period in the red.

SPAR's ability to pick valid medium term futures turns can be seen by its signals, 75 percent of which saw the worst futures drawdowns in the first trading month after each trade. Only four of 32 completed pairs would have achieved lower levels later than 20 days after the transaction (not shown). None of those pairs exceeded the worst 20-day single mark of a 20.9 point loss in October 1990. A total of five trades had draws of more than 10 points within 20 days, but only two were losers at the 20-day mark and then by only three days in each case. And the record gets better. Ten of the 35 short-term trades saw drawdowns of zero or less than one point, and most were substantial winners at 20 days. In short, the futures record for SPAR is favorable for those traders with deep pockets (and steeled nerves).

**TABLE 4–1  S&P 500 Continuous Futures with SPAR Signals, 1982-93** (Results During Following 20 Sessions and Next Opposite Signal)

| Date/Signal | Price | 20 Session High | 20 Session Low | 20 Session End | Next Opposite Signal/Result |
|---|---|---|---|---|---|
| **1982** | | | | | |
| April 23 (Sell) | 119.65 | Apr.26 120.55 −0.90 | May 19 114.65 +5.00 | May 20 114.95 +4.70 | August 3 105.45 +14.2 |
| August 13 (Buy) | 104.85 | Sept. 3 123.10 +18.25 | Aug. 16 103.30 −1.55 | Sept. 10 119.65 +14.80 | Nov.11'83 167.85 +63.00 |
| August 16 (Buy) | 103.30 | Sept. 3 123.10 +19.80 | Bought@ 103.30 — | Sept. 13 124.10 +20.80 | Nov. 11'83 167.85 +64.55 |
| **1983** | | | | | |
| June 2 (Buy) | 164.45 | June 21 172.65 +8.20 | June 8 160.95 −3.50 | June 30 170.15 +5.70 | Nov. 11 167.85 +3.40 |
| November 11 (Sell) | 167.85 | Nov. 29 168.75 −0.90 | Dec. 9 165.30 +2.55 | Dec. 9 165.30 +2.55 | Aug. 1'84 154.85 +13.00 |
| **1984** | | | | | |
| August 1 (Buy) | 154.85 | Aug. 21 170.00 +15.15 | Bought 154.85 — | Aug. 29 168.10 +13.25 | Apr.25'85 184.20 +29.35 |
| **1985** | | | | | |
| April 25 (Sell) | 184.20 | May 20 190.40 −6.20 | May 1 179.25 +4.95 | May 23 188.75 −4.55 | Aug. 8 189.10 −4.90 |
| July 12 (Sell) | 194.60 | Jul.17 197.60 −3.00 | Aug. 7 188.20 +6.40 | Aug. 9 188.70 +5.90 | Aug. 8 190.10 +4.50 |
| August 8 (Buy) | 189.10 | Aug. 21 189.75 +0.65 | Aug. 16 186.75 −2.35 | Sep. 5 187.75 −1.35 | Dec. 13 213.40 +24.30 |
| December 13 (Sell) | 213.4 | Jan. 7'86 216.05 −2.65 | Jan. 10 206.35 +7.05 | Jan. 10 206.35 +7.05 | Jan.13 207.40 +6.00 |
| **1986** | | | | | |
| January 13 (Buy) | 207.4 | Feb. 10 217.55 +10.15 | Jan. 22 202.80 −5.60 | Bought 217.55 +10.15 | Mar.19'87 296.00 +88.60 |
| April 8 (Buy) | 235.6 | Apr. 21 242.25 +6.65 | Apr. 9 235.35 −0.25 | May 6 237.25 +1.65 | Mar.19'87 296.00 +60.40 |
| **1987** | | | | | |
| March 19 (Sell) | 296.0 | Mar. 24 304.20 −8.20 | Apr. 14 280.00 +16.00 | Apr. 16 288.90 +7.10 | Apr. 30 289.50 +6.50 |
| July 29 (Sell) | 317.05 | Aug. 25 338.40 −11.35 | Sold @ 317.05 — | Aug. 26 336.00 −8.95 | Nov. 30 232.00 +85.05 |
| November 30 (Buy) | 232.00 | Dec. 23 254.70 +22.70 | Dec. 3 223.60 −8.60 | Dec. 28 246.30 +14.30 | Oct.17'88 278.25 +46.25 |
| **1988** | | | | | |
| January 15 (Buy) | 251.50 | Feb. 12 258.80 +7.30 | Jan. 20 243.40 −8.10 | Feb. 12 258.80 +7.30 | Oct. 17 278.25 +16.75 |
| October 17 (Sell) | 278.25 | Oct. 21 285.00 −6.75 | Nov. 11 274.05 +4.20 | Nov. 14 268.85 +9.40 | Nov. 30 273.05 +5.20 |
| November 30 (Buy) | 273.05 | Dec. 19 282.10 +9.05 | Dec. 2 272.50 −0.55 | Dec. 28 280.35 +7.25 | May 26 '89 322.60 +49.55 |

**TABLE 4–1** *continued*

| Date/Signal | 20 Session | | | | Next Opposite Signal/Result |
|---|---|---|---|---|---|
| | Price | High | Low | End | |
| **1989** | | | | | |
| February 27 (Buy) | 289.00 | Mar. 16 | Mar. 1 | Mar. 27 | May 26 |
| | | 303.85 | 288.20 | 294.2 | 322.60 |
| | | +14.85 | –0.80 | +5.20 | +33.60 |
| May 26 (Sell) | 322.60 | Jun. 23 | May 31 | Jun. 23 | Jul. 23 |
| | | 332.00 | 321.45 | 332.00 | 321.95 |
| | | –9.40 | +1.15 | –9.40 | +0.65 |
| July 3 (Buy) | 321.95 | Jul. 31 | Bought @ | Jul. 31 | Jul.12 '90 |
| | | 348.3 | 321.95 | 348.3 | 369.45 |
| | | +26.35 | — | +26.35 | +47.50 |
| October 31 (Buy) | 343.15 | Nov. 27 | Nov. 6 | Nov. 28 | Jul.12 '90 |
| | | 346.70 | 333.40 | 346.55 | 369.45 |
| | | +3.55 | –9.75 | +3.40 | +26.30 |
| December 20 (Buy) | 347.85 | Jan. 3'90 | Jan. 17 | Jan. 17 | Jul.12'90 |
| | | 361.70 | 338.75 | 338.75 | 369.45 |
| | | +13.85 | –9.10 | –9.10 | +21.60 |
| **1990** | | | | | |
| May 4 (Buy) | 339.90 | Jun. 1 | Bought @ | Jun. 1 | Jul. 12 |
| | | 363.55 | 339.90 | 363.55 | 369.45 |
| | | +23.65 | — | +23.65 | +29.55 |
| July 12 (Sell) | 369.45 | Jul. 16 | Aug. 6 | Aug. 9 | Oct. 1 |
| | | 372.30 | 334.40 | 341.40 | 318.25 |
| | | –2.85 | +35.05 | +18.05 | +51.20 |
| October 1 (Buy) | 318.25 | Oct. 2 | Oct. 11 | Oct. 29 | Aug.14'91 |
| | | 318.35 | 297.35 | 304.00 | 391.20 |
| | | +0.10 | –20.90 | –14.25 | +72.95 |
| October 26 (Buy) | 306.25 | Nov. 19 | Oct. 29 | Nov. 23 | Aug.14'91 |
| | | 321.15 | 304.00 | 315.50 | 391.20 |
| | | +14.90 | –2.25 | +9.25 | +84.95 |
| **1991** | | | | | |
| January 17 (Buy) | 332.00 | Feb. 13 | Jan. 22 | Feb. 14 | Aug. 14 |
| | | 370.25 | 329.85 | 365.35 | 391.20 |
| | | +38.25 | –2.15 | +33.35 | +59.20 |
| August 14 (Sell) | 391.20 | Aug. 29 | Aug. 19 | Sep. 11 | Dec. 16 |
| | | 397.00 | 378.85 | 384.70 | 386.65 |
| | | –5.80 | +12.35 | +6.50 | +4.55 |
| December 16 (Buy) | 386.65 | Jan.2'92 | Dec. 19 | Jan.13'92 | Jan.13'93 |
| | | 420.35 | 384.60 | 415.80 | 433.35 |
| | | +33.70 | –1.95 | +29.15 | +46.70 |
| **1992** | | | | | |
| June 15 (Sell) | 411.6 | 413.0 to 6/30 buy 401.3 | | | |
| Jun 30 | | | | | |
| | | | | NA | 409.5 |
| | | –2.60 | +9.70 | | +2.10 |
| June 30 (Buy) | 409.50 | Jul. 14 | Jul. 7 | Jul. 28 | Jan.13'93 |
| | | 417.70 | 407.95 | 417.40 | 433.35 |
| | | +8.20 | –1.55 | +7.90 | +23.85 |
| **1993** | | | | | |
| January 13 (Sell) | 433.35 | Feb. 4 | Jan. 20 | Feb. 10 | NA |
| | | 449.55 | 433.15 | 447.10 | |
| | | –16.20 | +0.20 | –13.75 | |
| August 16 (Sell) | 452.35 | Aug. 31 | Sold @ | Sep. 13 | NA |
| | | 463.35 | 452.35 | 462.85 | |
| | | –11.00 | — | –10.50 | |
| October 28 (Sell) | 468.05 | Nov. 16 | Nov. 4 | Nov. 26 | NA |
| | | 469.45 | 458.40 | 463.15 | |
| | | –1.40 | +9.65 | +4.90 | |

The record also makes an important long-term point for institutional investors. There were 15 short sales (all sells were shorts) included in the futures record and 20 buys; 12 of the sales were completed with a following buy by year-end 1993. Since the single long-term error was a sale, we have a 91.7 percent success record for potential long-term hedging of long portfolios and the 20 buys were error free. Given the preponderance of S&P rising periods compared with declining periods from 1982 through 1993, this record is highly significant. The record was extremely variable in the short term, but SPAR's long-term futures hedging record certainly deserves consideration.

# Short-Term Timing

What can be done to improve short term timing? The way SPAR patterns are formed and an outside indicator play important roles.

First, consider sell patterns. As noted in Chapter 2, all SPAR sell patterns require upticks in smoothed breadth to be triggered. Two also require gains in the S&P. So each sell pattern will arise only when the market is improving from recent levels. "Improving," however, is a relative word. A sell may come near a recent low or at a new high. The patterns alone don't differentiate between them, opening an opportunity to improve or confirm short-term timing.

The obvious point to observe first is whether the S&P itself tells a story: Is it near a low in both time and distance when a SPAR sell is signalled? If so, a delayed sell action is sensible. If the market has had a notable short-term run before the signal, it is better to take the sell action soon. This obvious reading create a correct frame of mind for action; further observations create more precision.

The 1993 sell patterns are excellent examples (all are closing prices). A short-term setup sell pattern came on January 13 with the nearby S&P futures at 433.35. Only three sessions earlier, it had reached an interim low of 429.10, clearly a near term low that cast doubt on a quick sell action despite the fact that with nearly all SPAR patterns of this type the market corrected to below the signal level within 20 trading sessions. Here, the contract did correct to below the signal level five sessions later, but by only 0.20 points.

More significant was the shape of the SPAR pattern itself. Going into its internal makeup, the smoothed advance–decline (ADS) minimum component line was stuck at −128 from December 16, 1992, indicating no serious breadth decline for nearly 20 sessions to January 13, 1993. Was one due? ADS itself showed an interim low on January 8 and was rising steadily by the sell on the 13th, four sessions later, suggesting that a breadth dip was likely to be on the way but not immediately. Thus, while both the SPAR pattern and the S&P suggested that investors wait, the question was how long?

I advised clients to take profits on January 18th, the first down day in ADS and the S&P after the signal with the S&P at 437.30. Since the advice came with the Stock Model still fully bullish, the signal was a mild sell. As it turned out, clients gained nearly 1 percent in the S&P from the delayed sell, but it was 12 points or 2.6 percent too early. The February 4 high was 449.60, after which the market bounced around its highs until the 15th when the S&P 500 lost nearly 12 points and the DJIA lost 82 points.

The whole period from January 13 through February 15 was therefore three sessions longer than the 20 sessions from the signal date that I have used for measuring short-term success of S&P 500 futures trades. Nevertheless, the setup sell signal lived up to its correction promise, and a slightly delayed short sale on January 18 made it profitable within the next 20 sessions. By using another outside indicator, this was improved further.

The SPAR sell on August 16 was of the ordinary variety, and the market behaved similarly to that of January. From an interim low of 448.65 on August 5, the S&P futures rebounded to 456.30 on the 18th. The ADS minimum component line was again stuck, this time at −159 from July 22. ADS itself had hit an interim low on the 12th and since risen. The period was a carbon copy of January as far as ADS was concerned and the Stock Model was bullish.

Result: clients were advised to make a moderate sell into the rally but to do so within a week of the August 16 ordinary sell signal, which brought a futures high of 461.05 and missed the actual interim peak on August 31 by 2.3 points. The ensuing correction took the Dow off 115 points by late September and the S&P futures a smaller 1.6 percent. As in February, the September correction ended 23 sessions after the first signal in August, but still within 20 sessions of the delayed action date. Under these rough guidelines, the futures short sale was profitable. The model accurately called for the correction to be modest.

The October 28, 1993, SPAR sell was again a short-term setup, but this time the internal pattern was different. First, the S&P futures had reached a record high on October 15 at 470.35 and closed at 467.70 on the 28th. Meanwhile the ADS minimum, which had held at −259 from the September 21 low through October 18, ran out of its allotted time window. It then upticked to −52 and dipped to −129 just two days before the signal. This provided a highly unsettled pattern that could be interpreted to go either way. The pattern could have been in the process of setting new lows or it could be reversing course to an upswing. In either case, the bullish Stock Model expected the correction to be mild.

The market moved quickly to an interim S&P futures low on November 4 at 458.40, then failed to rebound well on the North American Free Trade Agreement (NAFTA) vote and corrected again; within 20 post-signal sessions, the best S&P futures level was 467.10 on November 15. By year-end, two months after the signal, it had topped the signal level by only 4 points at its peak and was again below it. At a minimum, the SPAR signal and Stock Model expectations had been met, with only the short-term timing in doubt due to the unsettled pattern.

We can do still better in timing. Outside the SPAR system, the stochastic indicator is exceptionally useful in short-term timing. The indicator was designed for this sort of timing problem, when an investor knows what to do and how much capital is necessary but wishes to capture the best short-term price while acting. The knowledge derived from SPAR eliminates the major stochastic shortcoming: longer-range forecasting capability. We can concentrate on its strength for the short term.Stochastics reveals when price momentum is being lost on rallies and is gaining after declines. ADS also measures these facts for breadth, but with some lead to the S&P. We thereby have a theoretically potent pairing: the highly reliable SPAR signals and the stochastic momentum change in the S&P cash or futures.

I have tracked the stochastic record back to fall 1988 on the Fast-Track database[1] with 14-day stochastic timing and a five-day MA trigger for the S&P 500 *cash* (see Table 4–2). The table covers 19 SPAR signals, eight of which were sells, but one was interrupted with a buy signal before 20 days (June 15–30, 1992).

---

[1]Investors FastTrack, 11754F S. Harrell's Ferry, Baton Rouge, LA 70816.

**TABLE 4–2   SPAR Signals with Stochastics, 1988–93**

| Signal Date | S&P Cash | Stochastic Trigger | | +20 Sess. S&P | Gain/Loss |
|---|---|---|---|---|---|
| | | Date | S&P | | |
| **1988** | | | | | |
| October 17 (Sell) | 276.4 | Oct.26 | 281.4 | 269 | +12.4 |
| November 30 (Buy) | 273.7 | Immediate | | 279.4 | +5.7 |
| **1989** | | | | | |
| February 27 (Buy) | 287.8 | March 2 | 290. | 294.9 | +4.9 |
| May 26 (Sell) | 321.6 | June 14 | 323.8 | 330 | (6.2) |
| July 3 (Buy) | 319.2 | July 7 | 324.9 | 344.3 | +19.4 |
| October 31 (Buy) | 340.4 | Nov. 7 | 341.2 | 346 | +4.8 |
| December 20 (Buy) | 342.8 | Dec. 26 | 346.8 | 330.3 | (16.5) |
| **1990** | | | | | |
| May 4 (Buy) | 328.4 | Immediate | | 367.4 | +39 |
| July 12 (Sell) | 365.4 | July 18 | 365.2 | 340 | +25.2 |
| October 1 (Buy) | 314.9 | Immediate | | 301.9 | (13) |
| October 26 (Buy) | 304.7 | Nov. 1 | 307 | 316.5 | +9.5 |
| **1991** | | | | | |
| January 17 (Buy) | 328 | Immediate | | 364.2 | +36.2 |
| August 14 (Sell) | 389.9 | Aug. 15 | 389.3 | 383.6 | +5.7 |
| December 16 (Buy) | 384.5 | Immediate | | 420.8 | +36.3 |
| **1992** | | | | | |
| June 15 (Sell) | 410.1 | Immediate | | interrupted | +2.0 |
| | | | | | at 6/30 buy |
| June 30 (Buy) | 408.1 | Immediate | | 422.2 | +14.1 |
| **1993** | | | | | |
| January 13 (Sell) | 433 | Feb. 11 | 447.7 | 449.8 | (2.1) |
| August 18 (Sell) | 456.3 | Sept. 7 | 458.5 | 461.2 | (12.4) |
| October 28 (Sell) | 467.7 | Nov. 3 | 463.4 | 463.15 | +4.5 |

## Comments

This record shows 14 gains in 19 buy or sell trades to fixed dates of 20 sessions, surely a good performance, given the rising market in which three of the five losses were from short sales. Further, four of the five losses were occasionally profitable *during* the 20-day holding period or, in the case of the October 1, 1990, buy, in 30 sessions. The following sessions were profitable when the trigger produced a loss at 20 sessions (from signal date):

    May 26, 1989 +2 to 7 trading sessions

    Dec. 20, 1989 +2 to 11

    Jan. 13, 1993 +2 to 16

    Aug. 16, 1993 +2 to 3, 10 to 14

Each short sale might thus have been covered at a profit within 20 days. The futures table shows that the October 1, 1990 buy was also profitable by a tiny 0.10 the day after the purchase.

Perhaps most important, the long-term record from Table 4–1 reveals that *none* of these trades showed a loss at the next opposite signal. Of course, this record covers a shorter period than the full futures table, but it's hard to argue with a perfect record for the 19 most recent short term trades over a five-year period.

It's also worth noting that the stochastic trigger worsened the price from the signal date on the five delayed buys, but it improved four sells and worsened three slightly. In bullish or neutral Stock Model periods, which all dates were, prompt action on all buys and delayed action on sells appears a sound general strategy with stochastics.

From this, two good rules of thumb can be created in SPAR signal–stochastic short-term timing when the Stock Model is bullish or neutral: (1) make all buys on the signal day or the next, and wait for the stochastic trigger on all sells, and (2) expect to cover short sales within a time window of 2 to 12 sessions after the sale. With this strategy, 18 of 19 short-term trades were profitable. Therefore, if no gains or losses were assigned to the above four covered trades as a result of acting during their profitable periods, the compounded cash gain was 376.5 percent versus 64.5 percent for an S&P buy–hold. This clearly should make the stochastic indicator the outside indicator of choice for timing SPAR futures trades.

Professionals who wish to hedge long-term portfolios should follow the same rules. The futures record differs from cash only in amount, not in success ratio. It was 92 percent accurate over the entire history of the S&P futures and 100 percent accurate over the past five years. In the latter, however, five margins calls would have occurred on the seven trades with stochastic timing. Yes, deep pockets are necessary.

# Options

The options market presents one significant and obvious problem to the SPAR/stochastics trader: the decaying time value of option premiums. This problem occurs because SPAR buy–sell and sell–buy trades have relatively long holding periods that vary greatly in length. This fact requires a complete option strategy that is beyond the scope of this book. However, it does suggest that the short-term trading ideas already discussed may well be profitable in a similar way with index options. Let's briefly consider a few recent examples under adverse market conditions without attempting to prove any future relevance.

Using the closing price for OEX puts on stochastic trigger dates for the three SPAR sells in 1993, on second or third out of the money strikes (depending on activity), with expirations the second calendar months after the trade dates, the price action matches the S&P cash quite closely (see Table 4–3).

Using the futures rule of thumb with these options and arbitrarily buying back the puts on the second day after purchase, the trades would have generated a profit of 6.63 points before commissions on

**TABLE 4–3    1993 OEX Put Options with SPAR/Stochastic Triggers**

| Date | Put Option | Closing Price |
|---|---|---|
| Index at 410 | | |
| Feb. 11 | April 400 | 4 7/8 Buy |
| Feb. 12 | | 5 1/8 |
| Feb. 16 | | 10 1/8 |
| Feb. 17 | | 9 5/8 |
| Feb. 18 | | 9 1/2 |
| Feb. 19 | | 8 1/8 |
| Feb. 22 | | 7 3/8 |
| Feb. 23 | | 7 3/4 |
| Feb. 24 | | 5 3/4 |
| Feb. 25 | | 5 |
| Feb. 26 | | 4 3/8 |
| Unprofitable thereafter | | |
| Index at 425 | | |
| Sept. 7 | Nov. 410 | 4 1/2 Buy |
| Sept. 8 | | 5 |
| Sept. 9 | | 4 5/8 |
| Unprofitable to: | | |
| Sept. 20 | | 5 1/2 |
| Sept. 21 | | 6 1/4 |
| Unprofitable thereafter | | |
| Index at 428 | | |
| Nov. 3 | Dec. 420 | 5 1/8 Buy |
| Nov. 4 | | 6 5/8 |
| Nov. 5 | | 6 3/8 |
| Nov. 8 | | 5 1/2 |
| Nov. 9 | | 5 1/2 |
| Unprofitable thereafter | | |

three puts costing 14.50, for a gain of 45.7 percent—certainly an adequate gain in three put trades into a rising market even though the first accounted for the bulk of the gain.

For my highly limited test, a single strategy had to be employed, but other option strike prices and expirations could be selected for any given SPAR signal with an option optimization model. Because this is outside the scope of the book, I suggest that options traders use their own optimization models to track the specific SPAR signals over the past 10 years to quantify results. The foregoing suggests that such research may well discover serious profit potential, despite my purposefully limited scope.

We have developed a worthwhile means of refining our short-term timing on the most recent SPAR signals. To be sure, it is not totally mechanical and requires some interpretation, but the strategic success of the process clearly suggests that long-term portfolio hedging by means of SPAR signals with futures and options is viable, and that short-term trading has significant potential. We are now ready to combine our SPAR research with the most pertinent strategies for stock selection, thereby providing a good indication of the full worth of the SPAR system.

---

### Author's Use Tip

Time is the key word to remember about SPAR use with futures and options. Don't overstay the short term, whether the trade is successful or not. SPAR has its greatest success rate within five weeks of its signals on both the buy and sell sides of the market. The statistical chance of the patterns being random then is one in over two million, but the odds fall to just one in 625 at three months. Take your best shots while you can. Or become a long-term portfolio hedger expecting to meet margin calls.

# 5 Mutual Funds, Individual Stocks and Timing

Thus far the individual SPAR patterns have been treated as essentially equal in risk and reward to one another. A dip buy is assumed to have about the same potential as a thrust buy and an ordinary sell has about the same value as a long-term sell. In order to determine more precise strategies, the various pattern types must be differentiated.

Table 5–1 summarizes the market results following each action pattern appearance during the period from 1980 to 1993. The numbers deserve study.

## Accuracy Summary

Table 5–1 shows a more detailed analysis of market action than prior summaries. For the sell group as a whole, the average maximum gain for all 20 signals up to 20 trading days was 2.0 percent compared with an average maximum loss within that period of 1.5 percent. By the next buy signal, the average was an overall gain of 6.4 percent, with an average loss of 3.7 percent between +20 days and the next signal. Thus, selling short over the short term was on average barely worth the risk, but by the next buy signal it was.

On the buy side, the 23 buys since January 1, 1980, generated an average maximum gain of 3.9 percent in the next trading month compared with an average maximum loss of 2.0 percent, for a nearly a two-to-one reward/risk ratio. At the next sell signal, the average gain was 18.9 percent, with an average interim loss of 5.0 percent. Both short term and long, following buy signals was well worth the risk.

The worst risk/reward of the specific types was the short-term set-up sell over 20 sessions, with a greater average loss than gain. This improves to a better than a 1.5 to 1.0 ratio by the next buy signal, but it is still the poorest signal. Why use it? Because,these results not only hide the important calls it made (e.g., February 1980 and March and July, 1987) but identifying profit taking opportunities before corrections is worthwhile when the signal gives no assurance whether the correction will be a minor or a major one.

The two other sells suffer from small samples and make generalizations difficult, yet they produced fine results from short positions in the

**TABLE 5–1   SPAR Pattern Accuracy Summary, 1980–93**

| | Average/Largest | | | |
| | Up to 20 Sessions | | Interim | At Next Opposite Signal |
| Type | Gain | Loss | Loss | Average Gain |
|---|---|---|---|---|
| **Sells** | | | | |
| 5 Ordinary | 2.3% | (1.1%) | (3.0%) | 7.2% |
| | largest | (2.4%) | (4.1%) | |
| 11 Short-term Setup | 1.1% | (2.5%) | (4.4%) | 6.7% |
| | largest | (4.1%) | (6.7%) | |
| 4 Long-term* | 2.6% | (0.9%) | — | 5.3% |
| | largest | (2.3%) | | |
| **Buys** | | | | |
| 7 Thrust | 3.3% | (1.5%) | (5.8%) | 11.3% |
| | largest | (6.1%) | (9.8%) | |
| 8 Dip | 4.2% | (1.0%) | (4.2%) | 19.7% |
| | largest | (2.7%) | (7.5%) | |
| 4 Waterfall | 4.1% | (2.5%) | (3.4%) | 20.3% |
| | largest | (4.4%) | (6.1%) | |
| 4 Major | 4.1% | (2.9%) | — | 24.3% |
| | largest | (6.6%) | | |

*Includes two signals in the 1970s and one same-sequence sell from July 1985 due to small sample size. The interim loss column shows the maximum decline during the period between 20 postsignal sessions and the next opposite signal.

short term. Their average long-term profit/risk ratio was a hefty four to one, which is remarkable considering that the period covered was the second greatest bull market of the century.

The best short-term performer of the group, although barely so, is the dip buy. To be sure, it garnered only a moderate profit ratio in the short-term, 4.2 percent versus 2.9 percent on average, but 4.2 percent is a very high average gain for one trading month in eight calls. Long term, it is the major buy's 24.3 percent average gain compared to zero interim losses that provides the best profit ratio. Both signal types are clearly outstanding.

The dip buy is also the most accurate of the signals, running only a 1 percent average short-term loss against a 4.2 percent average gain, with only a 2.7 percent average maximum loss. This includes the five exact lows it selected. Long term, it produced the second best risk/reward ratio at a 4.2 percent interim loss versus a 19.7 percent long-term gain, or nearly five to one. The dip buy generally trades off small, short-range errors for significant gains in the medium and long term. However, note the one 7.5% post- 20 session error.

The waterfall buy gets over any problems it might encounter quickly. Note again the small sample, but its largest short-term loss (4.4 percent) is greater than its short-term average profit. Still, its long-term ratio of better than six to one in profits over a 3.4 percent interim loss makes the waterfall buy number two among the patterns.

The thrust buy is the riskiest of the buy types because when it errs it blunders—witness the 6.1 percent largest short-term and 9.8 percent largest interim losses. Still, its average 20-day gain is twice as great as its average 20-day loss and it carries about that same risk for the long term. It is truly a bandwagon signal with all the potential timing risk that entails.

## Signal Types and Issue Selections

From the results, we can conclude briefly that on the buy side—with its modest short-term losses in the S&P 500—using above-average volatility issues for each buy makes risk sense. Using these issues is only slightly less appropriate for thrust buys. If investors have a 14 year historical record with a short-term market loss of only a maximum of 6.6 percent and a historical risk of less than 10 percent on a longer-range basis, it is certainly worth taking higher specific risk when the average potential gain is 19 percent. By higher specific risk, I mean selecting issues for use with SPAR signals that have betas or standard deviations above those of the market.

On the short sale side, skipping setup sells is justifiable because of their results, but using this type of signal to take profits on long positions is appropriate. The other two sells are historically far less risky, so short sales can be undertaken with them, although they should still be reserved for the stout of heart. Using the same signals for worthwhile profit-taking opportunities on long positions is definitely in order.

To estimate the value of this information, let's run limited tests through the period in which I've used SPAR in real time and two additional years so that we have a five year history for mutual funds. A shorter period will be used for individual stocks because the process of stock selection itself contains so many variables that little is proved by having a larger, longer-range list. My intent is to show the *potential* in using SPAR with mutual fund and stock records, not to prove their unquestioned validity.

To start, let's set a few criteria for issue selection. You'll want to use your own in the future, but these parameters should be considered because they fit well with SPAR's record.

## Mutual Funds: A Five-Year Record

One of the best ways, if not *the* best, to utilize SPAR signals is with mutual funds. Insofar as they are broad-based stock funds, mutual funds tend to reflect and should improve upon S&P 500 results. Moreover, when we have SPAR's track record, which outperformed the S&P 500 by four times over two decades measured in the S&P 500 itself, the implication is that professional fund management should be able to do better and perhaps significantly so.

I've selected a sample of results from three funds over the most recent five-year period for several reasons (see Table 5–2). First, a sample of three funds is sufficient because I'm not trying to prove that mutual funds will always outperform the market with SPAR signals. That isn't provable. Also, I'm not trying to pick the best funds for future use because market conditions and investment styles change nearly as often as socks. The best funds from 1989 through 1993 will almost certainly not be the best from 1995 through 1999.

My fund-selection criteria were modest: (1) a highest, five-star rating from *Morningstar Mutual Funds* at the beginning date, (2) one fund with a relatively high beta, and (3) only no-load funds that are open to all investors. Other investing styles and criteria may be more appropriate in the future.

I asked Morningstar's library to furnish the three top-rated funds that met my criteria, starting in the highest risk category for year-end 1988. The top three, however, were all relatively low beta funds with none above .80, thanks largely to the Crash of 1987, which, because of the risk-adjusted method used by Morningstar, rewarded lower-volatility funds in their five-year relative ranking. I used the two highest beta funds, Nicholas II and Windsor, and arbitrarily added another high-performing, high-beta fund (1.6), Berger 100, for comparison. The record shows that trades were made at SPAR signals, without the timing refinements discussed in the previous chapter. Capital gains are shown as paid and reinvested in new shares. The funds are all broadly diversified with three widely varying objectives: EQUITY, INCOME, and PURE GROWTH.The performance is measured using SPAR signals *with the addition of new money on each buy signal* during the difficult markets that prevailed from one and one-half years prior to and three and one-half years after the 1990 market top, including the bear market of that year. The observations raise a number of worthwhile points to consider for fund investors using SPAR.

Note that $1,000 plus all prior sale proceeds was invested in each fund at each SPAR buy. Sells were made in proportion to the number of sells in sequence, that is, all shares were sold when a single sell occurred, one-third were sold at each sell when three arrived in a row. The sell signal on June 15, 1992, omitted as insignificant, would have added slightly to total gains.

## Observations on Growth Fund Performance

The bottom lines of the summary are most interesting. First, the S&P buy–hold was beaten by the SPAR/S&P trades in the "S/P Gain" column, but not by much—eight percentage points or about 12 percent in actual gain. More might have been expected. This modest gap occurred in part because the S&P trades were averaged in sequence, thus reducing their compounding effect. But the small difference arose chiefly because a bear market occurred in only three months of the whole period. There wasn't much reversing of the trend for SPAR signals to work with when measured in the S&P itself during these five years.

As to the individual fund results the record is somewhat biased by the buying of new fund shares at the signals, even when the new capi-

**TABLE 5–2   Selected Growth Fund Performance At SPAR Signals, 1989-93**

| | | | Nicholas II | | | Windsor | | | Berger 100 | | |
|---|---|---|---|---|---|---|---|---|---|---|---|
| Date | S&P 500 | S/P Gain | Price | Shares | Value | Price | Shares | Value | Price | Shares | Value |
| 2/27/89 Buy | 287.8 | | $18.64 | 53.65 | $1,000.00 | $13.76 | 72.67 | $1,000.00 | $19.22 | 52.03 | $1,000.00 |
| 5/26/89 Sell | 321.6 | 11.7% | $20.48 | 53.65 | $1,098.71 | $14.50 | 72.67 | $1,053.78 | $22.63 | 52.03 | $1,177.42 |
| | | | | 0.00 | $1,098.71 | | 0.00 | $1,053.78 | | 0.00 | $1,177.42 |
| 7/3/89 Buy | 319.2 | | $20.37 | 103.03 | $2,098.71 | $14.70 | 139.71 | $2,053.78 | $21.95 | 99.20 | $2,177.42 |
| 10/31/89 Buy | 340.4 | | $20.96 | 150.74 | $3,159.50 | $15.17 | 205.63 | $3,119.45 | $26.10 | 137.51 | $3,589.10 |
| 12/20/89 Buy | 342.8 | | $19.60 | 201.76 | $3,954.49 | $13.03 | 282.38 | $3,679.39 | cap gn:$15.62 | 282.25 | |
| | | | cap gain:$2.67 | 6.90 | | $.85 | 14.52 | | $7.58 | 419.77 | $3,181.84 |
| | | | $19.60 | 208.66 | $4,089.67 | $13.03 | 296.90 | $3,868.59 | | | |
| 5/4/90 Buy (4 Buy AVE.) | 338.4 / 335.2) | | $19.44 | 260.10 | $5,056.29 | $12.47 | 377.09 | $4,702.32 | $7.78 | 548.30 | $4,265.79 |
| 7/12/90 Sell | 365.4 | 9.0% | $21.22 | 260.10 | $5,519.32 | $13.00 | 377.09 | $4,902.17 | $8.82 | 548.30 | $4,836.01 |
| | | | | 0.00 | $5,519.32 | | 0.00 | $4,902.17 | | 0.00 | $4,836.01 |
| 10/1/90 Buy | 314.9 | | $17.58 | 370.84 | $6,519.32 | $10.55 | 55.45 | $5,902.17 | $6.92 | 843.35 | $5,836.01 |
| 10/26/90 Buy | 304.7 | | $16.60 | 431.08 | $7,155.90 | $9.88 | 660.66 | $6,527.34 | $6.60 | 994.87 | $6,566.14 |
| 1/17/91 Buy | 328 | | $17.91 | 486.91 | $8,720.61 | $10.29 | 757.84 | $7,798.21 | $7.01 | 1137.52 | $7,974.03 |
| | | | cap gain:$.14 | 3.81 | | $.32 | 23.57 | | $0.59 | 95.74 | |
| (3 Buy AVE.) | 315.9) | | $17.91 | 490.72 | $8,788.78 | $10.29 | 781.41 | $8,040.72 | $7.01 | 1233.26 | $8,645.17 |
| 7/31/91 Sell | 387.8 | 22.8% | $23.56 | 490.72 | $11,561.34 | $12.32 | 781.41 | $9,626.99 | $10.17 | 1233.26 | $12,542.82 |
| | | | | 0.00 | | | 0.00 | $9,626.99 | | 0.00 | $13,542.28 |
| 12/16/91 Buy | 384.5 | | $24.18 | 519.49 | $12,561.34 | $10.86 | 9778.54 | $10,626.99 | $11.91 | 1137.05 | $13,542.28 |
| | | | cap gain:$.40 | 8.59 | | $.84 | 75.69 | | $0.17 | 80.20 | |
| | | | $24.18 | 528.09 | $12,769.14 | $10.86 | 1054.23 | $11,448.96 | $11.91 | 1217.25 | $14,497.40 |
| 6/30/92 Buy (2 Buy AVE.) | 408.1 / 396.3) | | $24.03 | 569.70 | $13,689.93 | $12.59 | 1133.66 | $14,272.79 | $11.10 | 1307.34 | $14,511.43 |
| 1/13/93 | 433 | | $26.15 | 17.43 | | $12.71 | 33.89 | | $13.94 | | |
| | | | cap gain:$.80 | | | $0.38 | | | $0.00 | | |
| Sell 1/3 | | | $26.15 | 587.13 | $15,353.46 | $12.71 | 1167.55 | $14,839.62 | $13.94 | 1307.34 | $14,511.43 |
| | | | $26.15 | 195.71 | $5,117.82 | $12.71 | 389.15 | $4,946.54 | $13.94 | 435.78 | $6,074.77 |
| | | | share bal | 391.42 | 10,235.64 | | 778.37 | $9,893.08 | | 871.56 | $8,436.66 |
| 8/13/83 S1/3 | 456 | | $26.35 | 195.71 | $5,156.96 | $14.69 | 389.18 | $5,717.12 | $15.71 | 435.78 | $6,846.10 |
| | | | share bal | 195.71 | $5,156.96 | | 389.18 | $5,717.12 | | 435.78 | $6,846.10 |
| | | | cash | | $10,274.78 | | | $10,663.66 | | | $12,920.88 |
| 10/28/93:S1/3 | 467.7 | | $27.17 | 195.71 | $5,317.44 | $14.91 | 389.18 | $5,802.75 | $16.59 | 435.78 | $7,229.59 |
| (3 SELL AVE.) | 452.2) | 14.1% | | 0 | $15,592.22 | | 0 | $16,466.1 | | 0 | $20,150.47 |
| | | | Amt Invest | | $10,000.00 | | | $10,000.00 | | | $10,000.00 |
| | | | Net Gain | | $5,592.22 | | | $6,466.41 | | | $10,150.47 |
| Total | | | Return | | 55.9% | | | 64.6% | | | 101.5% |
| | | | Fund Buy–Hold w. CG | | 64.1% | | | 32.2% | | | 75.3% |
| S&P Buy-Hold | | 62.5% | | | | | | | | | |
| Compounded @SPAR trades | | 70.6% | | | | | | | | | |

tal is subtracted at the end. Extra shares lever the results during rising markets between SPAR buys and sells, and rising markets characterized most of this period. But I've calculated performance this way for precisely that reason. Any strategy that purports to offer worthwhile market entry and exit points had better be able to improve on both an S&P buy–hold and a selected vehicle's own buy–hold results. Clearly, the type of fund used matters significantly.

Considering only buy–hold results compared with the S&P, (the last line) Berger 100 was the only one of the three funds to outperform both the S&P buy–hold and the SPAR-traded S&P. Nicholas II, the small capitalization stock fund, beat the S&P buy–hold modestly but not the traded results. Windsor beat neither, missing by a long way. Clearly Berger 100 was the big winner in this modest sweepstakes.

The results of the funds trading with SPAR and adding capital on the buys is significant. (Total return line.) Berger 100 again was the star while the other two lost to the S&P. The likely reason for this performance is most important. The Berger 100 fund and others that are relatively high in volatility change price more dramatically when the market changes than their lower-volatility peers. A correct market entry and exit strategy will exentuate the value of dollar cost averaging more with these funds as long as they move in the same direction *and when* the market does. The latter point created the relatively flat performance of Nicholas and Windsor compared with their buy–holds. The two funds often marched to a different drummer than the S&P because of their differing objectives. Small cap funds in general weren't winners throughout this period. The equity-income strategy of Windsor did not pay off quite as well as that of Berger in one substantial period: June 1992 to October 1993. Note the jump in Berger's share price compared with Windsor's at that time; Berger actually won the race with this spurt.

A comparison of Nicholas and Windsor alone shows the results of Nicholas's relatively poor performance in 1993. From January 1989 to October 26, 1990, and adjusted for the capital gain, Windsor's price fell 22 percent. Nicholas fell just 7.5 percent. This gave Windsor buyers a chance to acquire more low-priced shares than Nicholas buyers, and with the market higher at the period's end, it accrued nicely to their benefit. Still, Windsor's relatively poor buy–hold alone gives us another tip: It's an equity-income fund that bolsters stock income with bonds and notes. Usually that's good for share price stability, but not always, as we've seen during 1990's period of falling bond prices.

The lessons should be clear: (1) Funds with relatively high volatility that are broad-based equity growth funds and aren't side-tracked with differing objectives or styles (i.e., Berger 100) and to which investors add fixed capital amounts on SPAR buy signals should tend to make the best use of the SPAR strategy. (2) Funds that have differing objectives may still do well with SPAR, but if their volatility coincides with the market, they are likely to do better than those whose volatility leads or lags the market. SPAR is a market-based strategy, so the closer a fund comes to paralleling that—but with wider swings—the better it will perform in the long run.

Accordingly, when anticipating a solid bull market the qualities to look for in a fund using SPAR are:

• A high risk-adjusted rating from a fund service such as Morningstar, usually the top one or two categories (four or five stars).

• A high beta (with a good R2 to bolster beta reliability) among the highly rated funds.

• Either a pure growth or value strategy without additional objectives to provide high income or to concentrate in market sectors or on capitalization size.

• A no-load acquisition cost; if a load fund is used, ensure that you have a long-term objective.

• A means of acquiring the fund on the exact day or a day after a SPAR signal, which means either cash at the fund or you or your broker must wire cash.

In the end, this would seem to lead investors to high volatility (beta) mutual funds to use with SPAR. With SPAR's performance record, that's not surprising: go for the max. Of course, this approach will not make all investors comfortable, especially when the market hits sharp downdrafts along the way, but that's a simple problem to solve. Utilize a lower-beta pure growth fund or a growth and income fund that is rated highly by your fund service. This trades performance for stability. There's nothing wrong with a pure S&P index fund either. However, give any fund you select an ample time frame in which to operate; three years or more should be your minimum.

# Individual Stocks: Selected Performance

We can now go farther out on our equity-selection limb to individual stock selection. SPAR's total record indicates that, like mutual funds, certain aggressive criteria can be employed in the stock-selection process, assuming the investor finds the attendant greater risk suitable.

Two criteria are sufficient for a stock selection test, relatively high volatility versus the market (beta), and high, current relative strength. For a limited test I used a random issue-selection process within the criteria, which suggests *potential* performance rather than proof that it must occur. I chose the 18-month period from June 30, 1992, to year-end 1993. The first date was a SPAR buy signal and the latter served as a proxy for the October 28, 1993, sell. (The market was only 0.3 percent lower at year-end than at the sell date.) The period was one where the market rose at close to its historic average rate of about 10.8% per year.

For the measure of randomness in specific stocks, I used the NYSE and the Amex/OTC issues of *Daily Graphs* for July 3, 1992, with the specific criteria that a selected stock must have beta greater than 1.5 and a relative strength in the top 15 percent of all stock issues. These criteria were not easy to meet on that date because the market had just completed a six-month slide.

The stocks selected were random: the first stock from the front of each book that met the criteria, the first stock after the book's midsection insert, and the first stock moving forward from the back of the large-scale charts. The six stocks were American President Companies, International Game Technology, and United Healthcare on the NYSE, Adaptec and Midlantic Companies from OTC stocks, and Hasbro on the Amex. The results are shown in Table 5–3.

The S&P 500 gained 14.3 percent in the period, excluding dividends as was done with the individual stocks, making the average stock gain of 67.4 percent look rather dramatic as does the fact that no losses occurred in the six random issues. Obviously, many objections can be made about drawing any conclusions from the performances in Table 5–3. No such brief holding period nor as limited a sample can prove anything. Pure luck certainly played some role in the selection, despite an attempt at randomness. However, I doubt that choosing a long SPAR history period with, say, 100 high beta, high relative strength stock prices at the buy–sell dates would prove more. There are too many variables that come into play in stock price movement besides those being tested. Differing market volatilities, surprise events, and lack of actual randomness within the criteria are among them.

As with mutual funds the conclusions we can draw are modest. SPAR's performance and risk record, however measured, suggests that seeking higher volatility issues that are currently outperforming at SPAR buy signals can be most rewarding. If such criteria can be melded into your present sound stock selection methods, and you can afford the risk of such stocks, timing purchases on SPAR buys should improve results, although probably not with every trade.

**TABLE 5–3   Selected Stock Performance** (Prices From SPAR Buy June 30, 1992, to Year-end 1993)

| Stock | June 30, 1992 | December 31, 1992 | December 31, 1993 | Percent Gain |
|---|---|---|---|---|
| American President | $44.25 | $38.75 | $57.25 | 29.4% |
| International Game Technology | 13.19 (split) | 25.44 | 29.50 | 123.7% |
| United Health Care | 42.13 (split) | 56.88 | 75.88 | 80.1% |
| Adaptec | 23.63 | 26.00 | 39.75 | 68.2% |
| Midlantic | 14.25 | 19.88 | 25.50 | 78.9% |
| Hasbro | 29.25 | 32.63 | 36.25 | 23.9% |
| | | | Ave. | 67.4% |

# Module Three: Timing Strategies

While I've stressed that SPAR is not a market timing mechanism, this does not mean that investors cannot develop action timing with it. Following are my suggestions on how to accomplish this.

## The Sell Side

One major element of any selling strategy in stocks is early identification of significant bear market potential. The SPAR signals themselves do not do this, even though they have repetitively appeared near major market tops. The signals provide no clear forecast whether the next decline will be major or minor, or come sooner or later. The Stock Model gives strong indications, of course, but still does not offer good forecasts on which to act. The best example is July 1990, when the model was bullish and a single SPAR sell appeared very close to the top. It was taken mildly (see Chapter 3), but the following S&P decline was 20 percent. Could investors have known something more serious was developing before the Iraqi invasion of Kuwait took place? The answer is yes, with a little chart analysis. The results are most important for capital protection in the overall SPAR strategy. Let's begin by going back to 1972–73.

Figures 5–1 through 5–8 each show one important characteristic that tips off investors to significant danger ahead: a pair of breakdowns in the S&P 500 *after one or more* SPAR sell signals, where important *prior* S&P lows are broken. Let me stress that some interpretation is necessary for each chart, so precision cannot be as great as

**FIGURE 5–1    1973 Standard & Poor's 500**

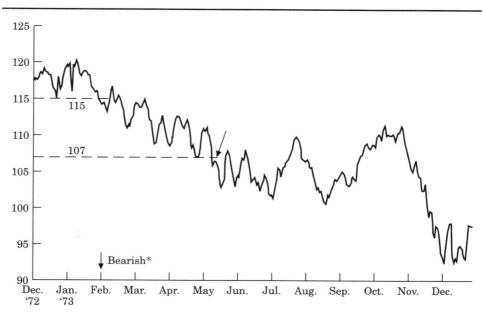

with the SPAR patterns. Nevertheless, each time a SPAR sell appears a major piece of information is given: a correction is coming; therefore, taking some profits will be a worthwhile action. A warning that the correction may become serious is generally given by an S&P break below its first prior prominent low.

In Figure 5–1, the two horizontal lines shown at S&P 115 (the December 1972 low) and S&P 107 (the October 1972 low) are the warning and danger levels, respectively. My rule would normally have been that the first S&P breakdown from the December 1972 low at 115 would be simply a warning, absent any other information except SPAR sell signals. (Recall that sells occurred in September 1972 at 111.5 and another in October at 110.) Positions were reduced accordingly. However, other information was available. The Stock Model had switched from bullish to neutral in August, which increased the sell signal's strength by one level according to Stock Model rules. Thus, there were three warnings (two SPAR sells and model downgrade) as the market rose to its January 1973 peak. Under such conditions, the February 1973 break of the first support at S&P 115 should have been taken seriously. A further warning: the Stock Model also turned bearish about the same time from an S&P moving average break.

Then came the second S&P breakdown at 107 in May. This "took out" the October 1972 major low and was the final danger sign. A sale that late would have missed the January 1973 high at 120 by about 10 percent, but look at the distance to the October 1974 low at 62!

The key point is that at each S&P break point more information was added to that already provided by SPAR and the Stock Model. The market itself was doing the talking. Taking such developments seriously is obviously warranted. This is a pattern seen in all subsequent charts of prominent SPAR sell signals.

**FIGURE 5–2   1976 Standard & Poor's 500**

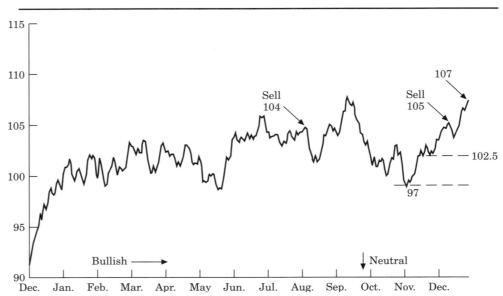

**FIGURE 5–2 (concluded)    1977 Standard & Poor's 500**

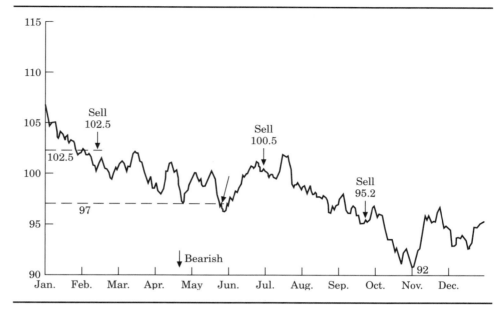

Figure 5–2 (left-hand panel) shows the 1976 market peak forma-tion and the two significant S&P lows that should have produced the warning and danger signals at 102.5 and 97. The first S&P warning came after two SPAR sells and a Stock Model downtick in February 1977 at S&P 102.5 along with a third SPAR sell (Figure 5–2, right-hand panel), that should have been a punch to investors' heads. But if it was missed, there was still the danger hit in May at 97.

Depending on how tightly one measured the May 97 break, sellers could have missed the rally to the July top amounting to just under 4 percent. The subsequent low at 87 did not take place until March 1978, but with all the prior attention-getters, only the truly blissful would still have been fully invested after the May 1977 message.

The year 1981 provides an instance in which the S&P warning and danger signals came a distance off the November 1980 record prior high at 140 (−7 percent), but the two did so only 3 S&P points apart (see Fig-ure 5–3). Again, with the prior Stock Model downgrades and March SPAR sell at 137, the 130 break in July was an ample danger sign. The September low was 112, nearly 14% below the 130 danger mark.

A similar situation existed in late 1983–early 1984 with a prior model downgrade in June and a SPAR sell in November (see Figure 5–4). By the time the S&P broke the October–December 1983 lows at 161 in February 1984 (and saw another model downgrade to bearish), the warnings were loud red. Note also the degree of prominence of the S&P 158 and 161 lows on the chart. The 161 level was a double low and 158 was a four-month low. The 158 break also came in February 1984. The difference this time was that the subsequent S&P low was only at 147 in July, some 9 percent below the 161 warning. I believe the warn-ing was still worthwhile, but you be the judge

A different picture appears in 1985 (see Figure 5–5). There was no

**FIGURE 5–3    1981 Standard & Poor's 500**

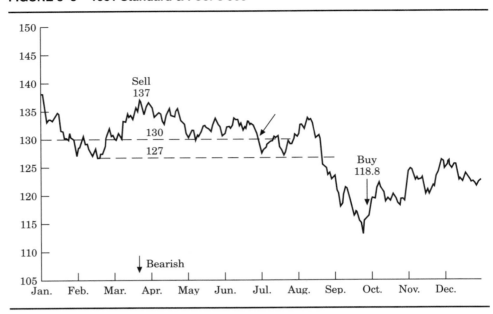

**FIGURE 5–4    1983 Standard & Poor's 500**

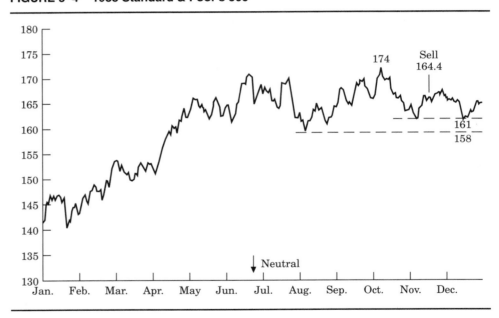

Stock Model downgrade and it remained bullish throughout the year. As previously discussed, the April sell was early, but under the model rule, it was taken mildly with the expectation of only a modest correction to follow. The sell in July was stronger than that of April and came very close to the interim top, but the Stock Model still wasn't fazed and stayed steadfastly bullish. That should have made any first S&P break suspect, but such concern was quickly obviated by the SPAR buy signal in August.

**FIGURE 5–5    1985 Standard & Poor's 500**

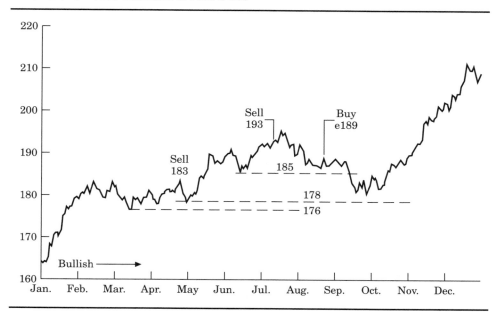

Frankly, I would still have been nervous when the S&P level of 185 was violated in mid-September. S&P supports are rarely broken just after SPAR buys, but the market action by early October 1985 confirmed that the March–May lows of 176 to 178 were not to be broken and the market was then rallying. The August buy was safe. I will return to this phenomenon with the "sell clearing" concept. For now, note that when SPAR and Stock Model signals are mixed, look to the Stock Model for the longer term and SPAR for the short term.

The infamous year 1987 yields yet another variation on the theme of double S&P warning (see Figure 5–6). With the SPAR sell March 19, the model downtick in April and the SPAR sell in late July, major warnings were flying and investors following the system were into the selling mode. Then came a series of market warnings, the first of which was at S&P 309, about 9 percent off the August 1987 peak, when the September low was broken. (Some chartists would have considered the break of the August low a few points higher as the first break, but it was so close to the double lows at 309 that it matters little.) The heavy 309 warning was unequivocal two weeks ahead of the crash.

Then the July low (not marked) and that of June at 303 were violated, thereby declaring loudly that major problems were afoot. If investors were still asleep after all this, the takeout of the major low of May at 277 was the wake-up call. Note its prominence on the chart. Investors would have had to act quickly though. The actual day of the Crash of 1987 was only three sessions away.

The year 1990 (see Figure 5–7) again offers a variation on the theme and brings us back to the original point in this strategy section. The market itself can tell great tales *when one is already alerted* to risks by SPAR and the Stock Model. Soon after SPAR sell signals are

**FIGURE 5–6   1987 Standard & Poor's 500**

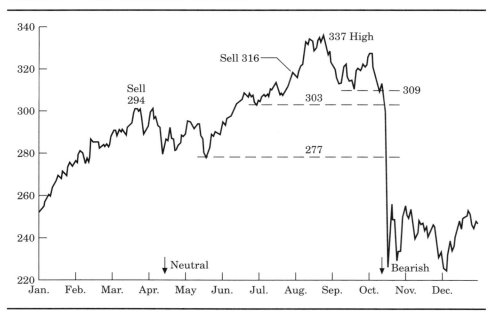

**FIGURE 5–7   1990 Standard & Poor's 500**

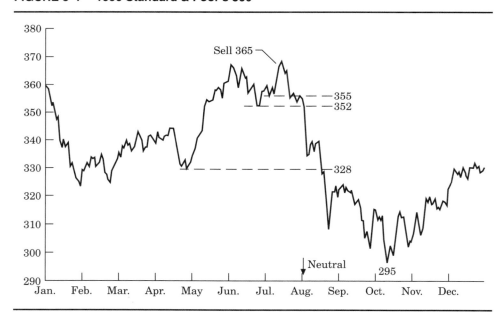

issued, alert investors can truly differentiate between unfolding high- and low-risk markets by market action itself. Remembering that there were few hints of the invasion of Kuwait until it happened, the S&P break of the minor low in early July at about 355 was the first warning after the prior SPAR sell. The Stock Model, however, was still bullish, as it was in 1985, so the S&P break was just that, a warning. Alert participants got their second warning soon afterward as the June low at

352 was broken at the start of the rapid plunge of the market caused by fear of war. There were two days for investors to act before the market hit the low 330s and rebounded—one day with a 351 close, the next at 344. The latter would have still saved 15 percent to the October low.

Inattentive investors would have gotten two more wake-up calls. The S&P moving average break and Stock Model downgrade at 344 and the takeout of the May low around 328 in August. Not much time was left to act, but savings were still to be had. The market had again trumpeted trouble in conjunction with SPAR and the Stock Model.

Only five other years saw SPAR sell activity since 1972—1980, 1982, 1991, 1992, and 1993. All but 1993 can be dealt with briefly and without charts. The SPAR sell near the February 1980 top in neutral Stock Model conditions was not followed by a break of the important prior low at S&P 98–100 before the waterfall buy in April.

The April 1982 sell with a neutral model reading was followed by the takeout of a minor low at 112 in May (also the September 1981 major low), so a protective sell then might have been in order. That was still 9 percent ahead of the final low and probably worthwhile saving. The break of the March 1982 low at 107 ahead of the August final low at 102 was more problematic and may have caused greater concern than necessary. The model was up to neutral as a result of a *downturn* in short interest rates in October 1981. That was a bullish development as the Federal Reserve was signaling an easier monetary policy. That policy had not changed by August 1982 and could have been read as a viable contrary model signal. In any case, the worry at this point was short lived. Two SPAR buys followed within as many weeks. The worst that would have happened was enduring a sell–buy whipsaw at 107-103. With the sell at a higher price than either buy, however, the resulting bother probably was insubstantial.

The year 1991 saw one sell signal before the Soviet coup in August. The brief ensuing market decline did not come close to violating any prior S&P lows and took place under bullish Stock Model conditions.

The brevity record-setting two week sell of June 15, 1992 also witnessed no market break of prior significant lows.

Let's turn to the most recent year, 1993 (see Figure 5–8). The significance of this year has already been discussed in terms of the SPAR sells into bullish model conditions, and I noted that the rules held true for the short-term corrections. Two points still need addressing: how to select important S&P prior lows as true support points and the "clearing" process whereby SPAR sells under bullish Stock Model conditions are closed out for the short term by subsequent market action.

The long, upward channel dating back to the April 1993 low is significant because it neatly contained the year's bull run. Every test of the rising top and the rising low was turned away. It is the archetypical picture of a self-correcting bull market, which gives us numerous S&P levels that must be violated before warnings and danger signals are generated.

Which are the significant prior lows? Look at Figure 5–8 again. Which are the most prominent downward spikes? Clearly the February

**FIGURE 5–8    1993 Standard & Poor's 500**

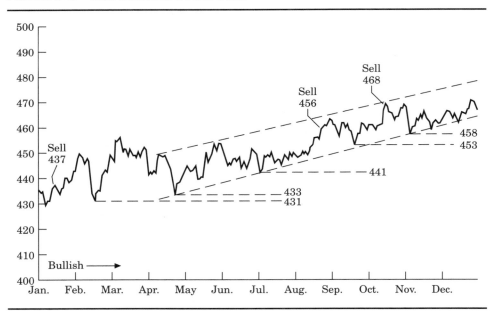

and April lows, then July and September, followed by the November–December series. Moreover, the November low near 458 was prominent because it was preceded by significant upside movement from the September low, which then becomes the next important low, and so forth. The more a low stands out from preceeding and following highs, the more significant it is. Double and triple lows are even more important.

The good news about 1993 is that unless the market is suddenly hit in the future with a huge one-day loss, there should be ample downside warnings. The market must proceed through many support levels before a true bear market trend will be confirmed. However, the uninterrupted occurrence of three SPAR sells, each with a minor correction, said that pressure for a notable down-move was building steadily, but the end of the bull market will truly be triggered by support breaks and the Stock Model. My advice is to take moderate profits at any subsequent SPAR sells but to expect only minor corrections until either the Stock Model downticks and/or violations of S&P prior lows begin. The first warning low is the part of November and September 1993 in the close range of 453-458. First true danger is a violation of the July low at 441.

The bad news is that the most likely changes in the model and market are likely to be caused by a Federal Reserve monetary tightening. Since nearly all market participants are highly attuned to this issue as a result of the Crash of 1987, when money tightening comes it is apt to cause a fast plunge. (See 1994 Update.)

Clearing SPAR sell signals is simple and fits with the foregoing. If a sell occurs under bullish or *upgraded* neutral Stock Model conditions, expect the correction that follows to be short term and mild, and to end at or just above one of the S&P's recent prominent lows. If the market follows this pattern and then rallies, consider the sell to be "cleared" for the *short term* of three to four weeks. If it then retests the prior low successfully or sets a new high, consider it cleared for the *medium term* of a few months.

This process worked well in 1993. After the February correction, the S&P rallied about three weeks, eased, and retested in April. After holding successfully above the prior low, the prior sell was cleared for the medium term and the market rallied steadily until after the August sell. During this rally the market made new highs and thus confirmed the prior clearing. Then, with the conclusion of the mild correction at the end of September, the market rallied about five weeks to the October sell, again setting new highs for confirmation. The market then corrected mildly again and held above the September low, thereby clearing the medium term. The market followed with a slow rally that still didn't top the prior signal level until January. When it did and made new highs, the prior clearing was confirmed.

Note that none of this fine-tuning cancels any SPAR signal, nor does it change the long-term cumulative effect of multiple sell signals, which remain in effect. If you want to think of this fine-tuning in terms of what power money is doing under these circumstances, it's simply taking short-term profits and making no attempt to forecast the market trend. This fits with what we've said previously about power money action. If you look back over the charts in this section, you'll find this process worked in all bullish model conditions when SPAR sells occurred. (They came in August 1976, April, July and December 1985, March 1987, July 1990, August 1991, and June 1992.) Even 1985 fit, despite the break of the prior low in August because that only became a brief "concern," not a point of action. SPAR can say a lot, but it can't eliminate concerns.

The bottom line in dealing with SPAR sells is to first take the action required by the SPAR–Stock Model interaction. If this arises from mixed readings, *expect* a mild correction and clearing, but let the market tell you what's happening. If the market clears the sell for the short or medium term, act accordingly. If it doesn't clear, wait for further SPAR, model, or market advice, which will come sooner than later. In addition, don't ignore the potential of cumulative SPAR sells. They say that market risk is increasing and it will be prudent to err on the side of caution by carrying smaller market positions but not moving out entirely. Finally, note that the foregoing sell strategy is consonant with our discussion in Chapter 4 about short-term setup sells, except that the strategy outlined here is broader.

## The Buy Side

SPAR buys require less additional information than sells to identify major market changes. This is likely a function of the market's historical upside bias and also the fact that one of the four patterns the waterfall buy—is searched for only after the market has taken a rapid 14 percent tumble.

The small sample makes generalizations about waterfall buys risky. However, one strategy that seems to eliminate most immediate downside risk is to delay the buy if the S&P is down from an interim high within the past two trading weeks (all but that of October 1974 were), and act when the short-term maximum ADS component makes its *second* new low. This strategy would have eliminated the minor 1 percent decline following the October 1990 buy and not made the buy price worse.

The strategy also would have saved five S&P points on the November 30, 1987 buy and caught the bottom one day and two points early. This idea also would have saved 3 percent on the downside at the October 1981 appearance but cost one point net. It would have saved 2 percent in April 1980 with the actual low the following day one point lower. In October 1974, the market was rallying strongly and had not come down from an interim high, so a buy would have been immediate. The 8.4 percent temporary loss to the December lows could not have been avoided.

As to the major buys, a rule of thumb I've tested is, on a signal date if the S&P is up more than 2.5 percent and three days from its two-week prior low, or the S&P is up more than 3 percent in three days or less, delay the buy until that prior low has been successfully tested. Successful tests are those that reach within 1.5 percent of the prior low and rebound for two days. Unsuccessful tests are breaks below the prior low by more than 1.5 percent. Successful tests should be bought on the opening of the third day, but unsucessful tests should be bought only when the S&P crosses above the prior low that failed.

By this rule, only two of the eight major signals would have required delayed buys: January 15, 1988, and October 1, 1990. The rules would have you buy lower than the price at the signal date by eight S&P points on January 22, 1988, and 12 points on October 15, 1990. Clearly, the delayed buys worked in these two instances.

As noted earlier in this chapter, the dip buy's timing is so precise that it has signalled buys since 1980 with no downside for the first trading month thereafter in five of its 9 appearances and has averaged only a 1 percent downside in that period. It hardly needs further refining. (See also the 1994 Update.)

The thrust buy appears to need further amplification. When it is analyzed closely, however, only one appearance was truly troublesome, that of January 28, 1982, which generated a 6.1 percent loss within 20 sessions and 9.8 percent loss before the next sell. No other thrust appearance showed a significant interim loss.

I find no peculiarity in the pattern that's common to this thrust appearance and lacking in the others. The interaction of the SPAR component lines, the Stock Model, and even the S&P's behavior are not sufficiently different among all thrust appearances to eliminate or modify action advice for any one. The best strategy for all thrust buys is to recognize that they arise when the market is already rallying significantly (3 percent to 5 percent from prior interim lows) and that this detracts from the potential gain ahead. Then follow carefully the Stock

Model's aggressiveness reading. It kept the January 1982 buy moderate. Expect that even if losses are shown temporarily, they will be recovered in due course. Recall that none of the SPAR buys showed more than a 0.25 percent loss at the following sell. Conservative investors also may wish to buy issues at these signals which are relatively moderate in volatility. Good relative strength readings in the issues selected also becomes more important.

The seasonality of SPAR patterns also deserves comment. The buy patterns for the period from 1972 to 1994 have appeared most frequently in October (six times), five times each in August and December, and four times each in January and April. Every other month is represented from one to three times. The relevance of this is that Octobers are widely known as one of the two worst performing months of the year, that is, good times to buy for the longer term. (September is the other.) August is the traditional summer rally month. December and January are year-end rally/January effect months. SPAR seems to know market traditions very well.

Clearly, timing strategies for SPAR signals are far less precise than the patterns themselves, due to their semisubjectivity. Timing is icing on the cake, but the SPAR-Stock Model interaction is a fine cake without it. Use the timing refinements as you see fit. More importantly, the system is sufficiently flexible so that most of its parts can be melded into your own investment strategies. This is particularly true of the mutual fund and stock selection criteria, and of the concept that all SPAR buy signals offer excellent "pitches" to hit, if investors know what to expect when they swing.

## Action Summary

In Chapter 1, I noted that the probability was high that the SPAR patterns themselves would continue to appear with similar market results in the future. The support for that statement comes from the statistical lack of randomness in the patterns, the continued performance of the patterns despite changes in power money's buy–sell strategies through the addition of program and derivative trading, and power money's continued use of its time-tested methods for moving blocks of stock.

Added to this is the fact that real-time use of the patterns has now gone on for four years and has covered a type of market not seen in the prior 20 years of pattern backtracking: the low volatility, low interest rate environment that has kept the bull market intact at levels of high valuation for over three years to 1994. Of course, this does not prove that the patterns must continue to repeat successfully. Nothing can do that, but the arguments in favor of the patterns doing so are indeed powerful.

My best guess is that new patterns will either be discovered or will develop as time goes on and the existing patterns will appear irregularly and perhaps less frequently. Since two patterns were discovered after 1990, the major buy and the rally stopper, certainly, complex computer analysis will locate others. Moreover, the long-term sell pattern has not made an appearance since 1985, which might suggest that its relevance is fading until it is remembered that the thrust buy did not appear for nearly seven years from 1984 to 1991 and then popped up three times in a row.

All of this is conjecture, of course. The best point that can be made arises from the inherence of SPAR patterns in the market. There is nothing artificial about them. They are caused by power money, the largest component of which is institutional activity. With continuing institutionalization of the market the principal driving characteristic of the past two decades, any change in market composition that will alter the SPAR patterns in aggregate will require a change in this driver. That may occur, but all that is currently in evidence is an increase in this institutionalization.

Table 5–4 provides a ready action reference to each of the SPAR patterns. Table 5–5 summarizes SPAR results in the S&P 500 by pattern type.

A final major point of the SPAR strategy is its usefulness in determining market trends between SPAR signals. This is accomplished

**TABLE 5–4   Action Summary**

| Pattern Type | Record | Action | Comments | Reference |
|---|---|---|---|---|
| **Buys** | | | | |
| Thrust | 7/8, average gain 10.8% in 6.9 mos. loss 1982: 0.3% | Immediate, no refinements | Typically occurs 3%–5% after rally starts | Pg. 21 |
| Dip | 13/13, average gain 19.1% in 8.7 mos. | Immediate, no refinements | Accuracy 1% short term | Pg. 23 |
| Major | 8/8, average gain 32.3% in 11.8 mos. | Delay on recent S&P trend, see p. 84 | Powerful pattern w. refinements | Pg. 30 |
| Waterfall | 4/5, average gain 25.8% in 12.1 mos. loss 1981: 0.2% | Conservative investors delay per p. 84 | Good bottom picker in bear markets, small sample | Pg. 25 |
| **Sells** | | | | |
| Ordinary | 5/5, Aug. 1993 incomplete at year-end. | See Stochastics timing | Small sample | Pg. 33 |
| Long-term | 2/3 | Stochastics timing | Small sample, highly accurate | Pg. 38 |
| Short-term Setup | 12/16, 2 from 1993 incomplete at year-end. | Stochastics timing | Don't short | Pg. 35 |
| Stopper | 25 appearances | Not an action pattern | The rally stopper | Pg. 40 |

**TABLE 5–5  SPAR Signal Results by Type to Next Opposite Signal**

| Buy | | | | Sell | | |
|---|---|---|---|---|---|---|
| Thrust | Dip | Major | Waterfall | Ordinary | Long-term | Short-term Setup |
| 5/72 4.8% | | | | | | 9/72 41.7% |
| | | | | | | 10/72 40.9% |
| | | 10/74 60.6% | 10/74 47.5% | | | |
| | | 12/74 55.1% | | | | |
| | 2/75 24.9% | | | | | |
| | | 4/75 24.6% | | | | |
| | 7/75 17.6% | | | | | |
| | 12/75 18.9% | 12/75 18.9% | | | | |
| | 3/76 3.4% | | | | | |
| | | | | | 12/76 2.4% | 8/76 1.7% |
| | | | | | 6/77 –2.1% | 2/77 –0.1% |
| | | | | | | 9/77 –7.8% |
| | | | | | | 2/80 11.7% |
| | 8/80 12.0% | | 4/80 33.6% | | | |
| | | | 10/81 –0.2% | | 3/81 13.3% | |
| 1/82 –0.25% | | | | 4/82 12.4% | | |
| | 8/82 58.2% | 8/82 58.0% | | | | |
| | 6/83 1.1% | | | | | |
| | | | | 11/83 6.3% | | |
| 8/84 19.0% | | | | | | |
| | | | | | | 4/85 –3.1% |
| | | | | | | 7/85 2.2% |
| | 8/85 11.0% | | 11/87 20.1% | | | |
| | | 1/88 9.7% | | | | |
| | | | | | | 10/88 1.0% |
| 11/88 17.5% | | | | | | |
| | 2/89 11.7% | | | | | |
| | | | | | | 5/89 0.7% |
| | 7/89 14.5% | | | | | |
| | | | | 12/85 1.5% | | |
| | 1/86 42.3% | | | | | |
| | 4/86 26.0% | | | | | |
| | | | | | | 3/87 21.7% |
| | | | | | | 7/87 27.1% |
| | | 10/89 7.4% | | | | |
| | 12/89 6.6% | | | | | |
| 5/90 8.0% | | | | 7/90 13.8% | | |
| | | 10/90 23.8% | | | | |
| | | | 10/90 28.0% | | | |
| 1/91 18.9% | | | | | | |
| 12/91 12.6% | | | | | | 8/91 1.4% |
| 6/92 6.1% | | | | | | 6/92 0.5% |
| | | | | | | 1/93 –7.7%* |
| | | | 8/93 –3.0%* | | | 10/93 0.3%* |

TOTALS (Number, Average Gain)

| Thrust | Dip | Major | Waterfall | Ordinary | Long-term | Short-term |
|---|---|---|---|---|---|---|
| 8: 10.8% | 13: 19.1% | 8: 32.3% | 5: 25.8% | 5: 7.1% | 3: 4.5% | 16: 8.3% |

*To year end 1993

through the ADS line based on its historical shapes. Part II covers this analysis in detail. I've set it in a separate section of this book because understanding the ADS line requires chart analysis, something not all investors are comfortable with or interested in. *However, this analysis is not required for using the SPAR patterns or the system just described.* Study or read Part II as you wish, but note that it can provide an excellent feel for the market when SPAR patterns have not appeared for a time.

---

**Author's Use Tip**

The short-term timing methods are truly refinements in the SPAR picture. They are not to be considered as inherent modifications. SPAR is not subjective at all. But timing is, because in one form it uses another measure for evaluation—a market index—and requires investors to determine where "prominent" support levels are. In the timing cases where one or more SPAR parameters are utilized, the parameters require interpretation. SPAR signals do not. Keep these distinctions clear and the timing ideas can correctly be seen as potential aids to, not changes in, SPAR actions.

---

# CHART ANALYSIS

# 6 Module Four: A Practical Further Step

This chapter moves us into SPAR's contribution to the interesting world of short-term market forecasting and trading. The analysis is based on charts that admittedly are less precise than SPAR's pattern signals. This analysis utilizes the smoothed advance-decline (ADS) data with which I worked for a decade before discovering the SPAR computer patterns. ADS has limitations, but it does provide valuable short-term market trend projections between SPAR pattern appearances. Combined, ADS and SPAR patterns contribute significantly to market insight. Working with them, you should be able to participate in almost every market move of more than 5 percent to 6 percent, SPAR's "noise" level.

## Using Chart Analysis

Chart analysis can also aid in short-term timing of movements into or out of the market called for by your independent fundamental or technical strategies, to form a stronger market picture at any given time. You can put the analysis to use immediately, without waiting for a SPAR pattern to appear. Chart analysis is an art more than a science, and it requires some study and exercise. I believe you'll be happy with how little.

Recall that ADS is an oscillator that moves from positive to negative numbers representing overbought and oversold levels as it measures the momentum behind market breadth. The principal value of ADS is its frequent ability to forecast days ahead the trend in the S&P 500 Index.

As explained earlier, the basis for ADS and the SPAR patterns is the daily net NYSE advance–decline balance, the number of advances less the number of declines. Figure 6–1 reprises this balance for early January 1992 as ragged line A. To better determine its trend, I have used a standard front-weighted smoothing, an exponential moving average, shown as line ADS.

To develop your own advance–decline smoothing, calculate the average of five days of net advance–decline (A–D) results and give it a weight of 75 percent. Then add the next day's net A–D to it with a 25 percent weight. The result will yield the smoothed ADS that is used for

FIGURE 6–1   January 1992 NYSE Advance-Decline with Moving Average

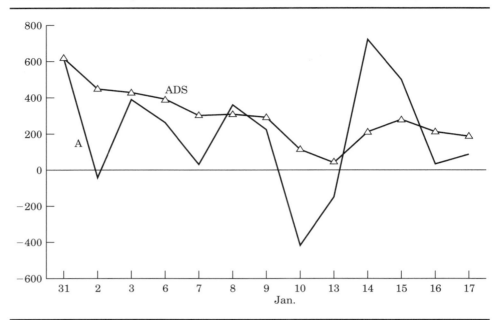

charting. On each day following, multiply the prior day's ADS by 0.75 and add it to the product of the new day's A-D net times 0.25.

A few guidelines are in order. First, using an ADS chart of less than six months in length tends to obscure the big picture and create a focus on the more errant short-term formations. A six-month to one-year length is ideal and the latter will be used in forthcoming examples.

Second, remember that NYSE breadth is not a market index. If that seems obvious, it still has an important ramification in translating the ADS motifs into market forecasts. Breadth, and therefore its smoothed cousin ADS, can change quickly from up to down, which can be successful in calling the S&P trend. It seems that the direction of ADS greatly influences forthcoming S&P movements. However, the steepness or slope of the ADS trend tells very little about the *magnitude* of the next S&P 500 index trend. In general, a steep ADS trend upward or downward does not usually equate with a steep follow-on S&P rise or dive. The contrary is often the case. In addition, a flat ADS trend does not necessarily mean a flat succeeding S&P move. I will note some exceptions, principally in determining how to spot a true ADS trend. Slope is not used to estimate the size of the following S&P move. Keep this distinction in mind, because it is very easy to wrongly anticipate the size of an S&P change from the ADS slope.

Third, as with standard technical analysis, the ADS charts have a limited number of motifs. The broad categories that appear most often are (1) "developing," those leading to an important market action, (2) "low risk," as the name implies, and (3) the type I call "believe" due to their extremely positive ADS readings and thereby investor tendency to doubt their longevity.

Fourth, the low-risk and believe titles imply that ADS has moved historically to regular extremes, and that's true. Only three times in the past two decades has ADS reached a level greater than +800 or −800. The first occasion came in October 1978 close to −900, the next in October 1987 when it exceeded −1150, and the last in August 1990 at −910. No positive readings exceeded +725. Thus, the expected ADS extremes lie in the + 800 to −1200 range. (See also Statistical Notes, Part I.)

Another boundary is of more practical importance. Figure 6–2 shows both ADS and the S&P 500 for 1992. This boundary is the set of horizontal lines marking reversal zones, or the overbought and over-sold areas. These exist because an oscillator must regularly reverse direction and the levels of +300 and −300 are rough demarcations of ADS *normal* reversal areas. The zones are not precise, but they don't need to be. Their purpose is to tell us when a given breadth trend is running out of gas for the very short term of a few days. By themselves, these levels say nothing about the medium or longer term. But, their existence yields important information when coupled with a longer running framework of one of the three ADS types, especially when ADS diverges from the S&P trend.

At the bottom of each S&P chart appear one or more of three terms: Bullish, Bearish, or Neutral. They refer to the Stock Model readings discussed in Chapter 3. The chart's plus signs and Buy or Sell notations refer to SPAR signals and their S&P levels.

Finally, all suggestions in Chapters 6 and 7 as to buy or sell points are not to be confused with SPAR buy and sell signals. They operate totally independent one another. Chart analysis is supplemental to, not part of the SPAR signals. And yet, you'll see they can work hand-in-glove.

In Figure 6–2, the steady decline in ADS from January into April along trendline *Aa* is one of the better formed, clearer patterns you will see. It is simply a series of declining highs as the shallow rebounds establish the trendline. When ADS showed important rebounds no less than four times as it approached its oversold level in April, it was acting normally. But note that the down trendline *Aa* was flattening from point 3 to point 4. Then the rebound at 5 didn't break up through it, and when ADS again turned down the result was the spike low to −500 and the fast rebound to the upper reversal area.

Meanwhile, note that the S&P trend steadily declined through the first three months of 1992. Despite the much steeper fall in ADS, the S&P wasn't reacting dramatically, a fine example of differing slopes for ADS and the market index, but not a divergence between the two: one up, the other down or flat. Instead, this picture was evidence of more and more declining stocks, but in most cases the declines were modest. The low in April was a "washout"—a steep oversold low—and cleared the air temporarily, as it turned out. ADS then shortly reversed its course near its upper zone.

As new trendline *Bb* developed in May and June at almost the same slope as *Aa*, it was accompanied by a flatter S&P than before, another example of ADS and S&P slopes separating from each other, but again with only a minor divergence: up compared with flat. With the third upside failure against *Bb*, however, the stage was set for

**FIGURE 6–2    1992 ADS and 1992 Standard & Poor's 500**

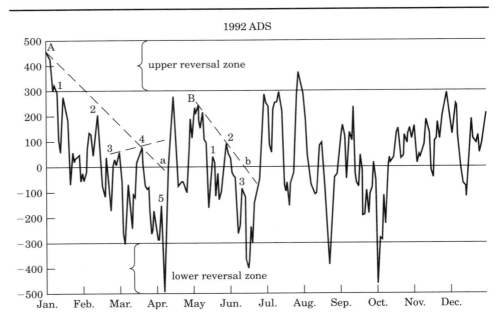

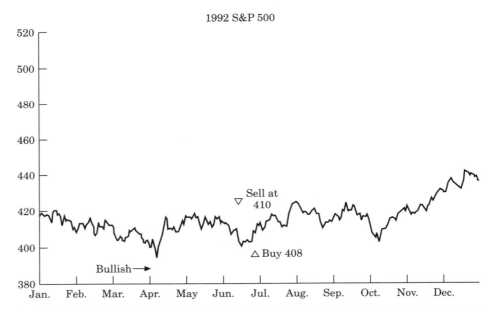

another dive into the lower reversal area, this time to around –400. It resulted in a more significant S&P reversal. Why?

Both the April and June 1992 S&P corrections were fairly mild. The reason for this has nothing to do with the ADS slope per se, which was down at about a 50-degree angle in both cases. Rather, the tip-off was the degree of *opposite divergence* between ADS and the S&P prior to completion of the corrections. The divergences were small, the worst being during May when ADS was down and the S&P was flat. Otherwise there was little divergence at all. The follow-up S&P moves were mild. This correlation, small divergence equals small following S&P moves, is important.

This leads to the first two ADS forecasting qualities, which will be tested on forthcoming charts. (1) ADS either leads or moves with the S&P on meaningful trends. It does not lag. (2) The greater any divergence between the ADS and the S&P trends in any given period of a month or more, the greater the magnitude of the next S&P move. That S&P move will be in the direction of the previous ADS trend.

In sum, three occasions in the first half of 1992 provided strong examples of the inclination of ADS to strongly reverse direction when it moved toward or into its reversal zones. On numerous occasions, ADS failed to reach those zones, and this led to weaker reversals. Most important, this motif appeared in the S&P index to a similar degree. The stronger reaction at reversal zones is typical of ADS configurations and is the most common set of conditions to appear in the ADS charts.

We also have seen the way ADS develops trendlines. When sufficiently extended, the trendlines can tip off investors to impending moves in the S&P. Despite the apparent steepness of a given ADS move, it is the divergence from the S&P trend that ultimately determines the magnitude of the S&P trend. In short, the first half of 1992 provides an excellent example of ADS actions to study.

Finally, the small triangles on the S&P chart in June 1992 shows the SPAR patterns of June 15 and June 30, the only SPAR patterns to develop during the year. The important point is that the ADS configurations we've just discussed had *little or nothing to do* with the arrival of the SPAR patterns. ADS provided the raw data, but remember that the SPAR patterns are derived from computer analysis of ADS internal parameters, not from the patterns ADS forms in the charts. Except by chance, the June, 1992 types of SPAR patterns will not have similar ADS chart setups in the future. Therefore, note that without further analysis ADS chart patterns do not forecast SPAR patterns.

## Developing Formations

The most common structure seen on ADS charts is "developing." In two examples for 1992 (see Figure 6-2), ADS first showed a downtrending parallel movement of lesser magnitude than the S&P, then trended downward compared with a flat S&P. Figure 6–3 shows a more important version of the ADS developing pattern, where ADS twice diverges sharply downward from a rising S&P in 1990.

After the late January to March ADS run-up that closely paralleled the S&P's rising highs, an ADS reversal came in March at point A. It occurred well below the normal +300 reversal zone, a sign of a continuing soft underlying market. Then a series of four fast ADS peaks occurred forming a downward trendline, while the S&P continued its rise.

**FIGURE 6–3    1990 ADS and 1990 Standard & Poor's 500**

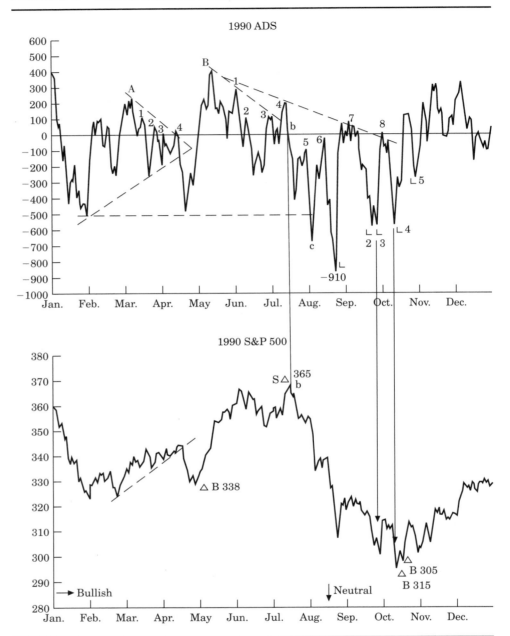

The magnitude of the March-April ADS/S&P divergence was noticeable in the series of falling ADS highs and rising S&P. However, note the difference between this formation and that of early 1992 in Figure 6–2. In 1992 both the highs and lows were falling. In 1990, they formed a symmetrical triangle. In standard chart analysis such triangles resolve themslves in sharp breaks either up or down as the apex of the triangle is approached in time. When ADS failed to rally meaningfully in April at point 4, a barely positive level, that should have correctly tipped investors that the S&P break would be down. Moreover, three or four prominent tests of an ADS trendline are about all it will stand for. However, there is an important variation: ADS requires a minimum of two points to form a trendline *after* a high or a low. In April 1990, there were four and the last broke the down trendline to the *upside*. ADS failed, however, to rise as far as the first declining peak—point 1—a motif that frequently repeats in ADS charts. As in 1992, when the trendline also is accompanied by a divergent S&P trend, danger is building, a hint that an S&P correction is imminent. The break in the upside trendline to a point *below* the trendline's first descending peak is a *false breakout*, a form of breadth failure.

False breakouts are defined as any third or later upside ADS movement that penetrates a declining trendline, but which fails to reach the highest declining point of that trendline. The greater the number of peaks that form the trendline prior to the false breakout, the better.

Therefore, in early 1990, there were clear tipoffs that an S&P sell-off of some size was developing: (1) the ADs symmetrical triangle approaching its apex, accompanied by, (2) a divergently rising S&P and, (3) a false breakout in ADS at point 4. The magnitude of the S&P correction can only be estimated to the degree that the longer the ADS down trendline takes to form, the more descending peaks it contains, and the more pronounced its divergence from the S&P, the greater the S&P fall is likely to be. As shown in Figure 6–3, any four-peak descent compared with a rising S&P is likely to be a tradable short-term S&P decline. In this case it was 5 percent.

This is a good point to note one of the imponderables in the ADS analysis. Determining exactly which short-term ADS move is the important break—false or otherwise—is subjective. For example, point 3 really qualified as a small false breakout. Point 4's was better. The only rule is that there must be at least two descending peaks after a high to form any trendline. On the other hand, a forecast of a market correction after point 3 wouldn't have long to wait for the real McCoy after point 4. All this is exemplary of the imprecision in ADS analysis. It's not a major flaw, but the ADS analysis does not provide the sharpness of SPAR patterns.

The next pattern is more dramatic. After the May 1990 parallel rally in ADS and the S&P, we again see a developing ADS structure appear to the downside, accompanied by an S&P slump in June. ADS then reversed slightly ahead of the S&P and for a brief period in late June rallied with it. By the time peak *B4* was clear following the failure of the ADS rally to top the peak at (B)1, one tip-off was given for an approaching S&P break: a false breakout. The fact that the S&P did reach a new high created the divergence factor and a sound reason to expect another market correction. At that point, no one would have known the magnitude of the slump to come from ADS alone. But a danger point was being announced, and the big picture ADS–S&P divergence was suggesting at least a correction of April's magnitude: 5 percent to 6 percent in the S&P. The arrival of a SPAR sell pattern just before point *b* (shown at the triangle on the S&P in Figure 6–3) made a quite strong sell argument.

This offers a corollary to our previous ADS observations. Since neither the parallel ADS–S&P modest correction in June 1990 nor the following June–July parallel rally changed the overall picture of declining highs from the May ADS top, the deteriorating ADS structure remained in force until after peak 8 (itself a false breakout). What we are seeing in Figure 6–3 is a complex set of smaller developing downside swings within a continuing larger one. Correct analysis of the short-term market trend would still have been for a correction at point *b*, a further decline after peaks 5 and 7, and another drop after 8. In other words, as each smaller pattern failed it contributed to a continuing failure of the larger one. It is important to be alert for these kinds of short-term swings in a larger ADS picture. Admittedly, this is one of the more "artful" aspects of ADS (or any other) charts. Being alert to the potential will help avoid forecast shock.

Before leaving summer 1990, when both the longer- and shorter-term ADS patterns were forecasting an S&P break of some significance (as was SPAR), we must note the major change in the ADS and market trend that took place next. The important features are that (1) ADS set one of its historic lows at –685 in early August, over two months before the S&P low in October, (2) that ADS low was followed by another even rarer low at –865 in late August, and (3) the S&P was not diverging with ADS, but had made a substantial correction. It lost 14 percent of its value just before the interim low in August. We'll come back to this latter point in a moment.

By the time ADS had failed at peak 5 and set the first rare low at point *c*, SPAR system investors would have been alerted that a major trend change was underway. The rest of the world discovered it with the Iraqi invasion of Kuwait on August 2, 1990. It pays to act on ADS–SPAR revelations even though the reasons behind them are not always apparent.

As stated in Chapter 2, any time the S&P has declined more than 14 percent within the short period of a trading month, it is susceptible to the formation of a valid SPAR buy pattern—the waterfall. The buy pattern formation occurs on the theory that such precipitous drops are not usually sustainable and, if they are, they exhibit a failed waterfall pattern (e.g., December 1973). Therefore, when a short-term drop of 14 percent occurs in the S&P, investors should not rely wholly on the ADS chart pattern to reveal a buying opportunity but wait for SPAR to signal the buy. It is usually too complex a situation for chart analysis alone.

Having said that, the ADS chart was in fact helpful. Let's look at a few telltale signs of an extreme ADS reversal. First, the ADS rebound from both of the extreme oversold levels in August 1990 was met with succeeding tops that remained within the down trendline from late April, forming prominent peak 6 and 7.

Then came the best clues. Two successive ADS lows were formed close together in late September, followed by another failed rally that was a true false breakout at point 8 from the long (from point B.) down trendline. The next decline also held around the –600 level, giving us a triple ADS low at L4. Close together triple lows are powerful formations to spot in the future. They are strong bottoming formations.

The next rally and low at L5 became a good test of the S&P's real low, since the ADS high was well above both peaks 7 and 8, and the L5 October low was above its prior lows. By the time of the SPAR waterfall buy signal on October 26, the ADS chart said a good S&P bottom was developing with a series of rising lows in both the S&P and ADS. Indeed, it appears from this analysis that the ADS chart successfully called the market low. (see also Chapter 7, Low Risk Formations.)

Unfortunately, other lows under waterfall conditions are far more complex and difficult to call from the ADS chart. Those of 1974, 1980, and 1987 were much more problematical. A comparison of those lows with that of October 1990 explains why I started more extensive analysis and discovered the SPAR patterns in the process. However, the ADS chart still provides guidelines that may be useful with other technical indicators in the absence of any SPAR signal.

I must stress that not all significant changes in S&P trends are preceded by "developing" ADS formations. There are two more types to address. However, it should be clear by now that multimonth developing structures that include increasing ADS–S&P divergence are worth serious attention, certainly if they are accompanied by one or more actual SPAR patterns.

The pair of figures from 1986 show a more complex form of ADS development (see Figure 6–4).

At the end of the strong parallel ADS–S&P runup in January and February (rising parallels signal a strong, broad market trend), the market became overbought with no less than five ADS peaks above +300. As technicians who use overbought-oversold oscillators know, this kind of extended overbought reading is not uncommon in broad bull market rallies. In this case, it was also preceded by a SPAR buy pattern in January.

Then the inevitable ADS deterioration began in February. The modest April S&P correction at point a was advertised by the three prior, prominent ADS peaks 1 to 3 that diverged strongly from the S&P trend. It was followed by a similar pattern in April. Then ADS went on to set a string of peaks—5 through 8. Note that peaks 7 and 8, which appear to be the start of an ADS rise, were accompanied by an S&P rally. But once the peak at 8 was clear two days later, the parallel move was clearly not a rally at all but part of a longer-range divergence. Peak 8 was well below peaks 2, 4, and 6. Granted, the 1986 ADS patterns were more difficult to spot than the neat patterns of 1990, but they were there nevertheless. The only missing element was the false breakout. The ensuing S&P correction from point d was 8 percent.

There is another point to this analysis, an apparent conflict between ADS forecasting S&P declines in April, May, and July, and SPAR's buy signal in April.

This isn't as discordant as it appears. It establishes another key point in ADS analysis. When SPAR patterns and ADS charts appear to conflict, SPAR is making a medium- to long-term call, while ADS addresses short-term opportunities. You choose which way to go,

**FIGURE 6–4  1986 ADS and 1986 Standard & Poor's 500**

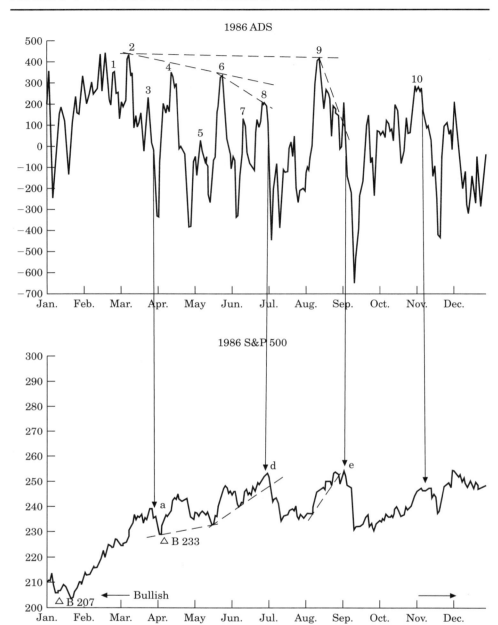

although the SPAR patterns are the more reliable. In this case, ADS provided short-term selling opportunities, each of which avoided the nasty S&P correction in July without giving up much. Longer-term investors were not hurt by a hold from the April SPAR buy. It turned out to be only 2 percent above even the September low. The apparent conflict between ADS and SPAR patterns was actually a difference in timing, not in forecast.

The August-November period in Figure 6–4 offers a good example of ADS chart variations. In this case, the ADS rules held true, but the picture developed very quickly. ADS breakdown from the overbought +450 level at peak 9 developed in only three weeks compared with the multimonth examples we've seen previously. However, the downtrend from peak 9 did have three succeeding declining tops and the last apparently broke above that trendline, only to fail quickly in a false breakout. This formation also came with an acute ADS–S&P divergence. Even peak 9 was below peak 2 in March. In short, all the ingredients for a danger sign were present; one had only to recognize them quickly.

This is where the slope of ADS is useful. True to form, it did not itself say anything about the magnitude of the next S&P move. That came from the very sharp ADS–S&P divergence just before *e*. Instead, the value of the ADS slope was in predicting a fast S&P move. It was worth recognizing: the S&P correction amounted to 10 percent. For future reference, the slope of the ADS decline from peak 9 is around 70 percent on the one-year chart for 1986, and it is accompanied by a *rising* S&P. That combination is worth identifying quickly, even though it is rare and has occurred only on a few occasions in the past 20 years, each of which was followed by a sharp S&P correction, including those of September 1973 and January 1983.

Care must be taken in observing ADS and S&P divergences. The March 1986 ADS decline from points 2 and 3 was accompanied by a generally rising S&P and was a divergence worth noting. But the April S&P correction was much milder than that in September. What was the difference? (1) The downward ADS slope was far steeper in late August than in March and the S&P rise was somewhat stronger in August. Thus, the divergence was greater in August. (2) The descending ADS highs in August established a good trendline whereas March saw an ADS collapse before a strong trendline could be drawn (only two minor highs between points 2 and 3.) Also, point 1 was actually part of the overall ADS motif at the time, making for a down-up pattern that was not as clear as that of August. These differences may seem small and they are not always easily identified, but they appear often in ADS charts and SPAR investors should be prepared to spot them.

An even trickier problem arose with ADS later in 1986. The ADS low of –650 in September was one of the extreme readings of the past two decades. As such it falls into our definition of *low-risk* formations, which are any ADS readings that move from a positive level to a negative 650 or lower. Low-risk formations are to be interpreted as part of good S&P *reversal* areas no matter what preceded them. (See Chapter 7) In this case, the S&P rallied briefly, fell to a second low about a point below that at the lowest ADS mark, and embarked on a significant rally to the March 1987 interim peak.

That's not tricky to spot, you say. In itself it wasn't. The problem came later in the sequence at ADS peak 10 in November 1986. The sharply rising trend from the September low was paralleled by the S&P, signifying a powerful market rally. However, the top at 10 should not have set off such a steep reaction. It wasn't forecast in the upside "developing" ADS–S&P run. There was no hint of deterioration in the ADS chart other than an ADS downleg that was developing to which the S&P made no reaction. Of course, the market slump after point 10 was caused by the surprise news of criminal charges brought against Ivan Boesky for insider trading. Thereafter, the market reversed quickly back to the old trend with a more modest correction. Still, the event reminds us that ADS can't forecast all market trends. Surprises will occur.

## ADS Developing Formations vs. SPAR Signals

The foregoing discussion brings out another key point. While ADS developing formations do often provide strong short-term market forecasts, they do not truly reveal strong action points. In contrast, SPAR patterns always issue action signals.

A good way to consider the difference between ADS developing designs and SPAR signals is that ADS should usually be acted upon by traders only, or when investors have other reasons for action. SPAR signals should be acted upon by both traders and investors. For example, if investors were waiting to add to stock positions in March 1986, they should have seen the start of the ADS breakdown at points 1 and 2 as a precursor to at least a modest S&P correction that marked a good time to buy while an existing SPAR buy pattern was operative from January. Waiting for the ADS low after 3 was certainly wiser than chasing the market to buy at almost any time in March. On the other hand, investors who wished to take profits in June after the big gains of the previous five months (and perhaps the steadily descending ADS highs at points 1 through 6), should have seen the rebound from the oversold June ADS reading as a logical target. Had investors acted on both the SPAR buy signals of January and April, they would have profits to take for the short term.

## Reading ADS Charts

A further example of the periodic complexity of ADS lows came in summer 1983 (see Figure 6–5). This is a fine illustration of a bull market that doesn't want to die.

First, January provides another extraordinarily steep ADS decline, even more rapid than that of August 1986. This time it was joined by a flat S&P. The following S&P correction didn't amount to much, about 5 percent. Why was it different from August 1986? The guidelines say (1) the ADS/S&P divergence was not directionally strong, a down ADS versus a flat S&P, (2) there were only two descending ADS highs after the peak, not three, and (3) there was no false breakout. When the breakdown was clear at point *a*, an astute forecaster would have said that a mild market correction was imminent—not large in percent—although it should be quick.

Then the first ADS high became part of a triple ADS top (points 1 to 3) set around the +450 level in January, March, and May. Distinct, separated triple tops are a worry on any chart, not only ADS. Note that in between the tops of both January and March–April, the declines had only two prominent descending highs followed by parallel ADS–S&P rallies. Clearly, they were not true developing weak patterns, and the market acted accordingly with a broad rise.

The triple top was then followed by a series of declining ADS tops, first with a quite steep slope (and a parallel S&P trend) in May from point 3 to a prominent peak at point 4. This was a stronger reversal than a false breakout and the breakout rules didn't really apply, although the rehearsal led to a minor S&P low in June and to a SPAR buy signal, one that was a bit early but just 2 percent above the August low.

This sequence led to another parallel S&P–ADS decline with a reversal peak in the point 5 formation. The small spike at 5, however, became a false breakout in the longer trendline marked by points 3–5. When the trendline was clearly established at point *b*, it set up the largest S&P correction so far that year, 6.5 percent. Admittedly, this picture is not one that ADS chart readers would have an easy time identifying due to its multiple interior formations. Nevertheless, our rules held. Were there not parallel S&P corrections within the development and parallel runs as the descending ADS peaks were set, this formation might well have led to a more serious correction.

Incidentally, the mid-July interim ADS low before point 5 looked pretty solid as it formed, and a buy on the rise to near the zero line would not have been seriously wrong, coming about 5 percent above the August S&P low. Note how the July ADS low was above that of June and it was formed with a jagged series of declines, which normally are fair indications that the steam has gone out of a market correction. But *important* market lows don't usually develop from ADS highs below the normal reversal zone, such as that at point 4, and especially following the barely positive peak at point *aa*. A fair reading of the conditions would have been, "OK to buy, but not brilliant."

Following this, we see a normal developing pair of structures forming: August and part of September to the upside, September through year-end to the downside. Both were accompanied by parallel S&P moves. Forecast: a good rally from the first—recall that upside parallels are strong markets—with only mild corrections to come from the September-yearend structure, and that was the way it turned out.

However, there is another feature of the 1983 ADS charts that is best seen by comparing ADS during the first half of the year with the last half. Before the late June ADS break, the great preponderance of ADS time was spent above the zero line, meaning breadth was highly positive. In addition, the S&P rallied throughout with very minor corrections. It was a powerful bull market. Contrast this with the second

**FIGURE 6–5  1983 ADS and 1983 Standard & Poor's 500**

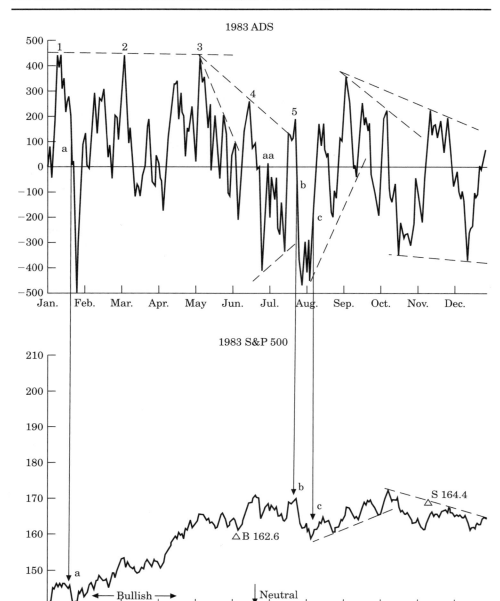

half of the year, when far more ADS time was spent below the zero line than above it. The S&P trend was (1) correction, (2) long but shallow rally, and (3) correction. It was a tough market to make money in, and it led of course to the minibear market of 1984.

The foregoing suggests that ADS charts have the capability to show market conditions over the longer term as well as the short. The first six months of 1986, with slowly deteriorating ADS tops and multiple reversals, were characteristic of self-correcting bull markets. In contrast, the first five months of 1983, with rare ADS forays into negative territory, showed a market about as strong as they come. However, when the May to August 1983 ADS deterioration set in, that picture clearly was changing. With the moderate downward slope in ADS and the parallel modest S&P correction, investors would have known that no major market break was imminent because no sharp divergence existed. But it would also have been known that market corrections of modest scope were to be expected, coupled with little upside progress. That's the hallmark of deteriorating ADS patterns with more time accumulated below zero than above. Note the ADS similarities between the second half of 1983 and April through August of 1986.

Back to 1983. There is a second theme late in the year, a series of declining ADS lows that accompanied the descending highs, the brief early November rally notwithstanding. The descending ADS lows were accompanied by a steady deterioration in the S&P from the October high, a parallel decline of nearly three months. This is the reverse of the January through March 1986 period. Since that period led to a continuing, if correcting, bull market, one would have expected the reverse pattern in 1983 to lead to the opposite, which it did. Again, I'm talking about the market's broad trend, not a short-term forecast. The appearance of a SPAR sell in November 1983 should have given ADS chart readers not only an action point, but also should have flashed danger signs when coupled with the developing negative ADS trend.

Finally, let's view a good upside pattern in the developing category, where a series of rising ADS lows combine with a flat S&P. October–November 1989 is a good example (see Figure 6–6). The October ADS low, caused by a program trading panic, was a spike in both ADS and the S&P. Interestingly, the preceding ADS formation had established the potential for this break with a series of declining tops, points 1 thorugh 7, the last of which broke the downward trendline, but failed to top the first declining peak. This was a false breakout with its negative short term implications. And, there was a moderate ADS-S&P divergence. An S&P correction was set up.

Next came the series of rising ADS lows, B1 through 3, as the market attempted to reverse course. This produced a trend *change* pattern: The S&P was in a downtrend until November, but the rising ADS lows were accompanied by rising ADS highs, a-c, which would have become clear around point 2. That was also when the S&P ended a brief divergence with ADS. At point 3 the rising ADS lows took hold and a short-term rally of 20 S&P points was ahead by January, suggesting that the ADS developing pattern forms similarly on the upside as on the downside. That is a good working hypothesis from the 20-year study I've made. However, finding good upside patterns with a clear downside divergence in the S&P is rare. Everybody seems to know when this bandwagon is rolling and the averages match breadth quickly. With a solid sampling of ADS developing structures behind us, let's summarize the qualities to identify as most productive in short-term forecasting.

**1.** A "normal" ADS high or low is one that extends into its respective reversal area, but not into the extreme areas of minus or plus 650. If it is normal in this sense, a developing pattern may be starting.

**FIGURE 6–6    1989 SPAR and 1989 Standard & Poor's 500**

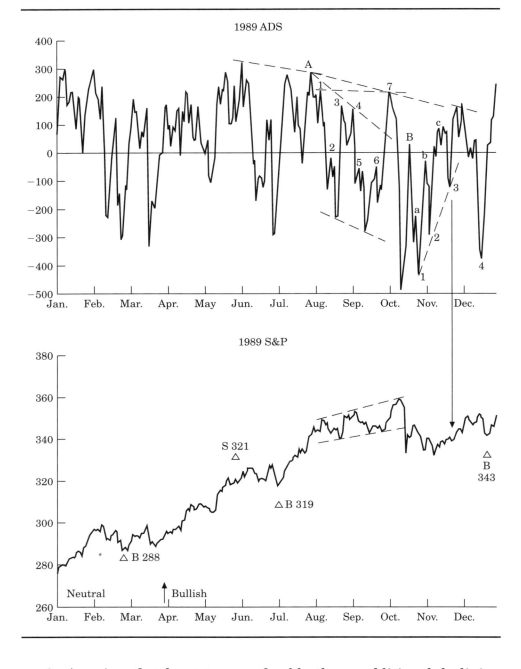

**2.** A series of at least two, preferably three, additional declining ADS highs or rising lows form a trendline. Their appearance says the development is proceeding.

**3.** Some degree of divergence of this trendline from the S&P 500 Index trend is necessary, at a minimum an up or down ADS versus a flat S&P. This should appear through most of the development period.

**4.** The critical point in developing ADS structures occurs when the ADS trendline is broken modestly in the opposite direction, but the break fails to exceed the first prominent point *on the trendline*. An S&P move is now imminent in the direction of the ADS trendline.

**5.** The steepness of an ADS decline is relevant only in the extreme, approximately like those of August 1986 and January 1983. Then expect an immediate S&P correction, but its magnitude is specified only by the degree of ADS–S&P divergence. The stronger the divergence, the larger the correction's size.

**6.** Developing ADS patterns set up *short-term* market reversals that usually last between a few days and a few weeks. Developing ADS patterns should not be used for longer-term market forecasts, with the exception of those that set market tone, the extended periods where ADS remains above or below the zero line.

The two more specialized ADS formations, "low risk" and "believe" are covered in Chapter 7. They offer greater precision in selecting action points.

---

### Author's Use Tip

One admonition that is most important in utilizing the "developing" chart formations is that investors not attempt to force an ADS chart to fit the examples given. Many graph structures begin like solid developing formations only to fail along the line. Recall that the purpose of finding valid motifs is to locate only those infrequent occasions when they say something useful, not to coax something out because you want to know now. Let the formations speak to you, don't ask them something.

# 7 Toward Greater Precision

## Low-Risk Formations

The second category of ADS patterns that have important market fore-casting capabilities are those reaching levels of a negative 650 or less. That's a quality that makes them very obvious to spot, but they provide readings contrary to their plunging appearances and are truly low-risk points in market trends. One must be very careful in determining when the development of these formations are complete to achieve the low-risk status. They are also quite rare as only 18 have appeared in the past two decades, with 13 of those accounted for by double and triple appearances in the same month.

| | |
|---|---|
| May 1973 | −740 |
| November–December 1973 | −653, −709, −658 |
| October 1978 | −911, −871 |
| October 1979 | −780, −700 |
| March 1980 | −770, −728 |
| September 1980 | −726 |
| December 1980 | −753 |
| September 1986 | −650 |
| April 1987 | −785 |
| October 1987 | −1167, −850 |
| August 1990 | −700, −910 |

The immediate features of the list are the six occasions in which two or three separate lows occurred below −650, all of which contained one level of −700 or lower.

This means investors should be aware that any ADS reading under −650 has the potential for setting a second low equal or greater to the first within a month's time, and that one of the two is likely to be below −700.

There also is a seasonal concentration of 14 lows in the fall from September through December, underscoring fall as a dangerous time for stocks. However, danger also represents opportunity.

Another fact—to recall from Chapter 6—is that four of the 11 periods shown also saw SPAR waterfall buy patterns begin to unfold: December 1973, March 1980, October 1987, and August-September 1990. That of December 1973 was rejected as faulty, however. All but one of the paired low ADS readings was followed within six weeks by the start of a market rally that exceeded 10 percent. The exception again was December 1973, but it saw a triple ADS low.

It should be clear that the low-risk ADS formations are among the most reliable short-term forecasters available. With a few simple qualifications, these deeply oversold levels offer excellent buying opportunities. Only one of them missed a worthwhile market low by more than a few percent.

One further observation. The –650 demarcation line for the low-risk category is precise. Variations above even –645 somehow don't work with the same precision. As the forecasting time frame suggests, these are low-risk buying opportunities, not *no-risk* chances. (See also Statistical Notes, Part I.)

## Examples of Low-Risk Formations

The first low-risk formation is October 1978 which provided a lovely forecast of an approaching market low in early November (see Figure 7–1). The low was set up by a proper developing pattern, where the sharp August ADS decline of three descending highs and a fourth that was a failed reversal became the danger point at S&P mark *A*, clearly a great point to sell.

The extreme –910 ADS reading came at point *B*, which was only about halfway down the sharp S&P slide. It was too early for the S&P low as the comments about the –650 appearances above suggested. That fact raises three useful observations: (1) There were no upticks in ADS after it failed in its October rally and broke the zero line to the downside; (2) the S&P plunge was parallel to the ADS dive; and (3) the ADS low was significantly below the low-risk qualification mark of –650.

As we'll discover with other low-risk examples, these qualifications establish a broad rule. When these qualities are met, expect the first rally or two in ADS and the S&P after the –650 or lower reading to be a "dead cat bounce," that is, a meaningless rebound. Too much damage has been done to the market from a technical standpoint to expect that traders' initial reactions will have set the real market low. The further below –650 the initial ADS low occurs, the more likely the S&P low is not set. Using caution is the best way to handle the probable double ADS low and avoid an early buy.

Second, ADS readings below –700 will usually be followed at some point—usually after a second low—by a series of rising lows, in effect a new developing structure to the upside. This is most often paralleled by an S&P rise. Careful investors will make purchases only after the new upward developing pattern appears with *at least* two rising ADS lows after the first low. That's when risk is indeed lower, even though

**FIGURE 7–1   1978 ADS and 1978 Standard & Poor's 500**

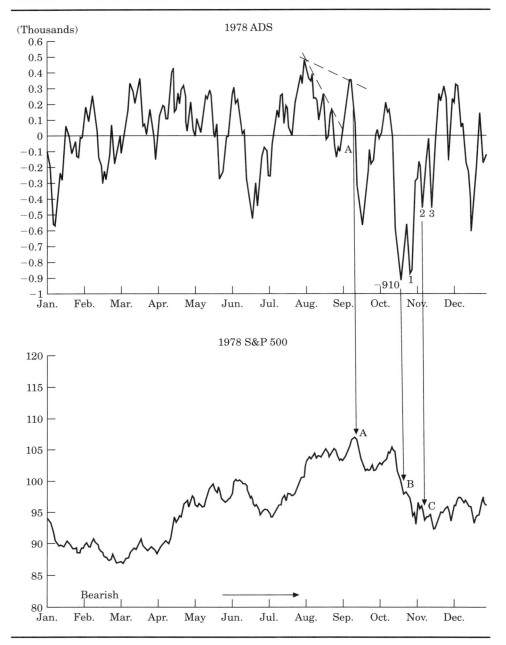

the S&P might be modestly above its actual low. (As we study more low-risk ADS formations, we'll make this rule more precise.)

In the 1978 example, this formation would have occurred in November at point *C*, not before, since that was the point where two ADS lows were higher than the lowest level. Being patient is the wisest course in buying near extreme ADS formations. The low-risk pattern requires the exercise of caution because of the high tension that pervades market psychology under breakdown conditions. It also can be highly rewarding when properly handled.

This strategy works best with ADS initial lows that are below −700, the further the better. The −910 of 1978 certainly qualifies. Naturally, life isn't quite this simple. What about initial lows that occur between −650 and −700? Or right at −650? Figure 6–4 for 1986 showed us one at −650 that was followed by a steeply rising ADS. The best S&P bottom was at the *first* rising ADS low, but the suggestion to wait for at least two rising ADS lows still applies for careful investors. Buying after even that second rising low in 1986 missed only about 3 percent in the S&P. You will see why the patience is worth it in two examples of this strategy from March and September 1980 (see Figure 7–2).

March 1980 provided a splendid example of the start of a complex market low, one that we noted earlier had triggered a SPAR waterfall buy pattern with an S&P decline greater than 14 percent prior to its conclusion (after the pinpoint SPAR sell pattern within two S&P points of the February high). The preference is to allow SPAR waterfall patterns that intervene with ADS formations to signal the actual buy. However, ADS alone again made a valuable contribution to identifying the S&P low with its pair of low-risk readings, separated by a series of dead cat bounces.

First, notice the steep ADS collapse in January 1980 was met with a sharply rising S&P between points *A* and *B*, yielding the best divergence yet seen and producing a classic example of a developing type danger signal, even to the point of a false reversal breakout at the February high (*B*). There could be little doubt about a forthcoming serious S&P correction following point *B*, notwithstanding the SPAR sell signal two days earlier.

Then ADS set its first serious low-risk mark at −770 and early on the S&P slump at point *C*. (The −610 low didn't qualify as low risk.) In doing so, note that ADS did not move from a positive reading to the low without an uptick day. That was an important warning the market low would not be an easy one.

Still, by the time the cat was close to resting with the succeeding −728 reading at point *D*, three separate higher ADS lows were in place after the −770. They had added a complication by descending 1–3, not rising as others shown earlier. They still worked, however, leading us to observe that as long as the lows following the −650 qualifier are *higher than the initial low*, they are acceptable. Only two minor S&P corrections were left before the market was off and running to a major 38 percent advance by November. (Note also the two SPAR buy patterns during the sequence.)

A problem still remains. I've said that buying the second higher low after the low-risk mark is sensible, and that patience in waiting for the end of the sequence is best. Which is it to be, the second or the end? The answer comes in the September and December 1980 ADS spike lows, both of which exceeded −725 and disappeared without cat bounces. September's dive was a pure surprise, with no developing negative ADS pattern ahead and a parallel fast S&P plunge. But the dive took place without a rising ADS mark from a positive level to the

**FIGURE 7–2  1980 ADS and 1980 Standard & Poor's 500**

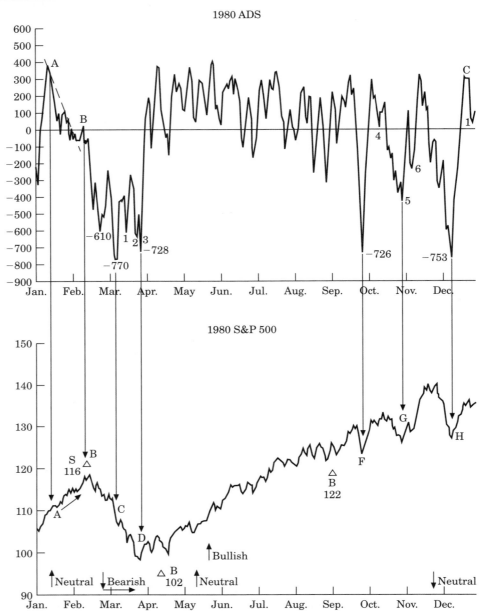

low, and it was completed so fast that it seemed to have been untradable with our low-risk rules.

The first higher low after the spike was just above the zero line at point 4 and the second came in October at point 5, this time well below the first. That provided two lows above the qualifying low but in descending order, the same variation the March 1980 sequence produced. Remember, they do not need to be ascending lows, but both must be at or above the –650 qualifying low. September and October 1980 demonstrated a test of the patience some ADS patterns require.

A clearer rule emerges from the March and September low risk qualifying ADS lows: When a descent from a positive ADS level reaches −650 or lower with one or more uptick days on the way, (as in March 1980), expect the final bottom to be complex and wait for a *third higher ADS low*, in whatever order, ascending or descending, it occurs. This would have meant a buy just after point D in April, but just after G in October with its no-uptick descent at the qualifying low in September. Some S&P distance was given up in each case but not much.

December's bottom was established by the very steep parallel downturn with a jagged descent in both the S&P and ADS, culminating in the −753 low. The jagged descent was again the tip-off to complex final lows. Waiting for a series of rising lows required even greater patience in the face of what appeared to be a runaway market in late December. Patience would have been rewarded in 1981, however (see Figure 7–3).

Buying the second ADS low in January 1981 at point *A* was contrary to the complex low rule. Doing so faced a six-point S&P downdraft (4.5 percent) before the final S&P low was set after point B. The December tip-off to a complex low would have avoided this early buy. Instead, making the buy after the third higher low at point *B* would have been about 3 percent above the final S&P low in February.

However, note that in both the October and December 1980 ADS low-risk rebounds, readings at the highest lows were *positive* twice at points 4 and C1. This was not true of rebound lows in either the March 1980 or the November 1978 low-risk formations, where they were at the normal reversal area of −300 or lower. After confirming this point in other low risk formations, we may add this corollary to the rule on which low to buy: If either of the first two rebound lows is above −200 do not count it. Then follow the applicable simple or complex low-risk rule to make the buy. That would have made the January 1981 trading buy at point C.

It should now be clear that ADS low-risk and developing category rules are quite capable of establishing good short-term buying conditions in markets that otherwise would be highly problematical. ADS greatest limitation is exactly what we should expect, that no two structures, even within the same category, are identical. The variations, no matter how small, would clearly lead to some uncertainty. Nevertheless, the rules are sufficiently tight to be workable for traders or investors who wish a more complete market reading in the absense of a current SPAR-Model signal. With this much background, we can turn to two of the most difficult apparent low-risk patterns, May and November 1973 (see Figure 7–4).

The May low at −740 was *almost* a classic for the rules, meeting all low-risk criteria with a third higher ADS low and a successful short-term buy at *A*, nearly the end of the six-month market slump.

However, several points are worth noting. First, the declining ADS highs (peaks 1–5) during the first five months of 1973 were paralleled by a declining S&P, thereby producing no divergence for a

**FIGURE 7–3   1981 ADS and 1981 Standard & Poor's 500**

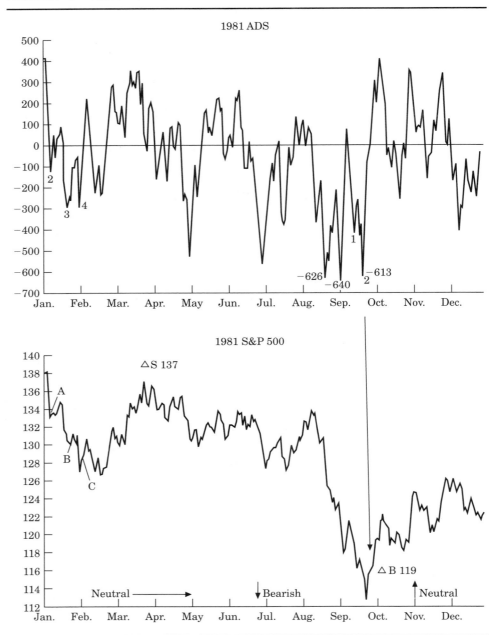

correct developing pattern and providing a disagreeable bear market tone for the entire period. Still, the break of the descending trendline at point 3 was a traditional false breakout with negative S&P implications.

The −740 low-risk spike with its uptick at the arrow, identified a complex low in process. By the time the third higher low at point 8 was clear, a trading buy was in order. It clearly turned out to be a short-term trader's buy with the market peak in July. However, there were other important imputs at point 8. SPAR had signalled two sells

**FIGURE 7–4    1973 ADS and 1973 Standard & Poor's 500**

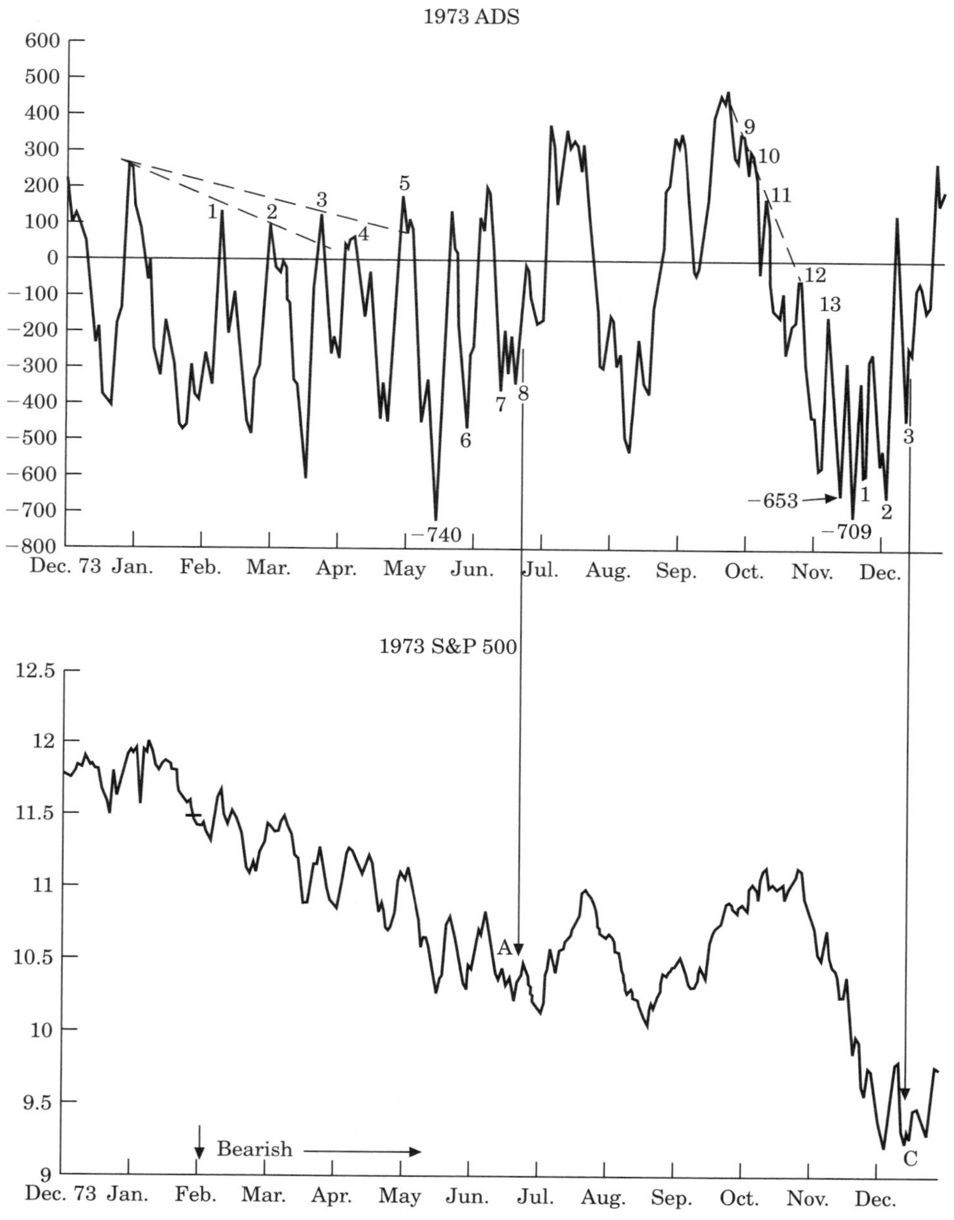

in fall 1972 and no intervening buy. The Model turned bearish February 1973. Even the S&P had signaled trouble with breaks of the prominent 1972 interim lows of S&P 115 and 107. All the flags were red. No trader should have expected more than a short term market stay at point A.

The November–December 1973 formation was established by a steep developing pattern diverging from the rising S&P. It was also a virtual photocopy of the August 1986 developing picture, except this one failed the final test where the last rising low at point 12 should have decisively broken the down trendline for a false breakout. When it failed, a careful trader would not have expected an early low. By the time the −653 low was set, the entire decline took on the aspects of a complex low where the minor peak at 12 was merely a violation of the simple low-risk formation rule that a move from a positive ADS level to the first low under −650 is to be accomplished without an uptick.

Over the next month, ADS established a −709 low and three rising lows with the second lower than the first. A buy following the third rising low would have been in order and would have snared the S&P very close to its low at point *C*, an apparently opportune call in light of an 8 percent run to the January 1974 highs. However, this took place in a monster bear market with the red flags of two prior SPAR sells in fall 1972 and a bearish model from February 1973. Traders should have again expected no more than a short-term trade. Indeed, no ADS selling pattern developed at those January 1974 highs (nor had they at the July 1973 peak.) Furthermore, the October–December S&P collapse met the −14 percent SPAR waterfall buy pattern trigger, but the pattern did not properly form before it ran out of time in January. From all standpoints, this was purely a trader's market, not one for long-term investors.

No discussion of major ADS lows would be complete without a serious look at those of 1987 (see Figure 7–5). ADS low-risk rules turned in a credible, if unspectacular, performance that year. The SPAR buy pattern was remarkable, however.

First, the April ADS low at −783 followed a three-month, by-the-rule, developing ADS pattern of no less than six descending highs. Point 5 qualified as a false breakout just after a SPAR sell signal, certainly a fine time to say adieu to the market for the short term. ADS then produced an additional declining peak at point 6, by which time the market trouble was obvious.

The April spike low at −783, was a classic with no upticks on the last leg down from point 6 in plus territory. It was a true low-risk pattern, followed by three rising lows, (a-c) the second of which was close to zero and violated the "two below −200" rule. That should have kept careful traders waiting for another low. Point d qualified for a buy at *A*, a bit off the S&P low but safer. A gain of 16 percent on the S&P lay ahead to the August high, with a SPAR sell signal near the end. Also note these points before the August top: (1) the divergence of ADS and the S&P between points 7 and 8, (2) the Stock Model downtick to neutral in April, and (3) the second consecutive SPAR sell signal in late July. As in 1973-74, red flags were flying.

The August top was followed later in the month by an ADS low at −644. But close doesn't count with ADS low-risk readings, and this is the best proof. This low was at the time a normal correction, followed by the start of a rising development pattern. All looked well until the peak at 10 was followed by a failure to top the point d rising low at point *e*. Matters were now getting dicey and traders following our rules would have understood that a potential serious low pattern was developing. That

**FIGURE 7–5  1987 ADS and 1987 Standard & Poor's 500**

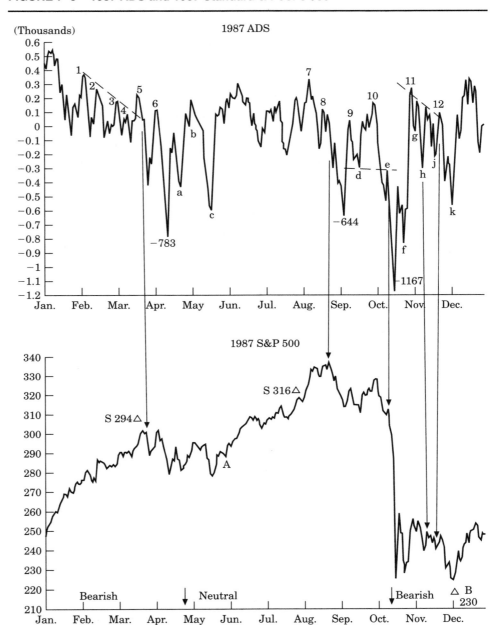

occurred three trading days before the Crash of 1987. The day after the crash, the complex low pattern became clear. The big low of October 19 set the ADS record at –1167 as befit the worst market break in a half century. Now it was a matter of waiting for the dead cat to do its bouncing. It did not do so perfectly.

Waiting for the third countable rising ADS low that the complex formation called for, eliminating point g as above –200, would have generated a buy after point j around S&P 242, some 8 percent above the final S&P low in December. A better buy point would have been after the fifth rising low at point k, but no low-risk rule would have called for it. Yet, there is an anomaly here. Note the descending ADS highs from point 11 formed a small developing pattern complete with a false breakout at 12. Unfortunately, just after point h this was only beginning. Alert traders might simply have waited longer in recognition of the crash, a once in a half century event.

However, investors would also have known a waterfall buy pattern was unfolding after more than a 14 percent decline in the S&P from the August peak—at the 280 level. Waiting for the waterfall buy signal should have been the paramount order. SPAR's signal appeared November 30, only two days before the actual S&P low in December 1987.

Finally, while dealing with low-risk patterns, let's return to that of 1990 (see Figure 6–3). With the addition of our low-risk rules, we now see a clearer picture. First, was August's –910 level a setup for a complex low? It was. There was no straight-line decline from a positive ADS level to that qualifying low, and the prior one at point *c* was also below –650. Therefore, a three-step pattern of rising lows would be required before a valid buying condition existed: the lows at points L2, L3 and L4. Again, the October SPAR buy signals should have been the operative factors, but certainly the ADS chart got traders in the right frame of mind, whether they got the numbering right or not. The ADS low-risk chart rules were again helpful.

## Low-Risk Rules

With our examples of low-risk ADS designs, we can now summarize the rules governing them.

**1.** To qualify as a normal low-risk type, ADS must generate a spike low below –650 after having retreated from a positive reading without an uptick day. Be wary of lows that are close to –650; even –640 does not seem to function reliably.

**2.** Assume that the qualified spike low is not the final bottom in that market move, but that a series of stabilization lows must follow.

**3.** Be watchful of the S&P 500 from its most recent prior high. It will often meet the SPAR waterfall buy conditions around to the spike ADS low. If so, let SPAR make the buy call.

**4.** If the waterfall test has not been met and the ADS spike low is indeed a qualified low-risk type, expect to buy when ADS has set two additional lows that are both higher than the low-risk qualifier and both are below –200.

**5.** If the ADS low below –650 is not a straight-line plunge or if the rising lows following it don't include two at –200, the pattern is a complex low. Then make a trading buy only after the third rising low.

Under these circumstances, according to theory—with its usual lack of guarantees—investors should be able to locate relatively low-risk buying opportunities in washed-out markets.

# "Believe" Formations

The final category of viable ADS patterns are those I have labeled "believe." They are the opposite of the low-risk formations in construction: high level, positive spikes. Contrary to their appearance, the believe formulations are almost invariably followed not by market declines, but by continued rallies. They are ADS version of the extreme overbought market that just goes rolling on.

"Believe" patterns are the surprise realizations the stock market gets periodically when it has either oversold the downside or reacts to a news event that makes the market suddenly undervalued at current levels. October 1974 gave us the first variety, the end of a grinding bear market that had been in force for nearly two years. Suddenly it was payday.

## Examples

Over the past two decades, there are seven months in which this motif appeared: January 1991 at +647; August 1984, +700; October 1982, +725 and +675; August 1982, +692 and +673; January 1976, +725; January 1975, +627 and +646; and October 1974, +641. Our examples begin with the rebound off the October 1974 market low. (The Dow Jones Industrials low came in December.) The characteristics are easy to spot (see Figure 7–6). ADS reached its peak on October 14, 1974, at +641 point $a$, and did so in a relatively uninterrupted run from a reversal low at –400 on September 30. The S&P low of 62.3 was reached during the ADS run-up on October 3.

Only two qualifications are needed for "believe" patterns: (1) that ADS reach a +625 level or greater, and (2) there must be fast run-up to the high with ADS at a negative level within 10 trading days prior to the spike. In October 1974, it was six days.

Like the low-risk patterns, this ADS formation is frequently associated with SPAR buy signals. A SPAR major buy came on October 7, a waterfall buy came October 14, the day of the spike high, and another major buy arrived December 10. In fact, all of the the "believe" buys except that of October 1982 came within a month of SPAR buy patterns. As with low-risk formations, if a SPAR buy pattern is in force at a believe spike, that signal should control action.

Timing believe buys is psychologically trickier than timing low-risk buys because investors must "believe" that the market is headed higher while it is very overbought and ADS is reacting negatively to the overbought spike. My primary rule is to expect to buy the day following the first day the ADS spike becomes clear. Because it takes a day to know that the spike has been set, the buy is actually the second day after the spike high.

In October 1974, the buy day would be October 16, two days after point $a$, or 70.3 on the S&P, which was the low until November 18. (The final secondary low was at 65 on December 6.) This buy did incur a 7 per-

**FIGURE 7–6   1974 ADS and 1974 Standard & Poor's 500**

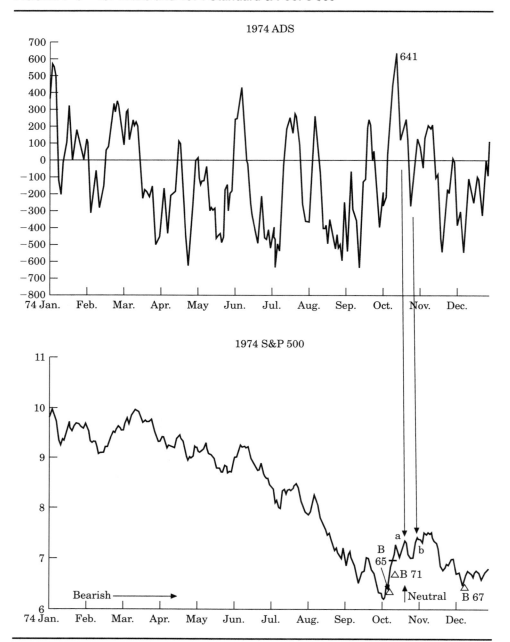

cent S&P loss by the December low—a more imprecise buy than ADS believers usually offer, but it was a rarity. Believe patterns have subsequently been more powerful, probably because market participants use more sophisticated tools and information inputs than those of a quarter century ago. Whatever the reason, believe patterns require fast action because of their power. They are markets not to be missed; our buy qualification of a second day's dip seems almost too long in hindsight. But even the sloppy 1974 buy produced an S&P gain of 25 percent in six months and 36 percent by the July 1975 interim market top.

Aside from the spike high, the other quality of believe charts is quickly obvious. Immediately after the spike, ADS starts an acute decline, one that appears to be a sharp developing motif to the downside. Ignore the normal interpretation of this formation. It's merely the inevitable fact that not every stock can rise day after day.

Contrarily, all reliable market reversals should be bought promptly—thus a second buy also can be made on the very next ADS reaction low. That would have been at point *b* in October 1974 which was still early. Again, this chart is a rarity. In Figure 7–7, we see a common addition to the explosive spike: a pair of tops at the ADS high.

October 1974 was not only the start of an extremely strong, broad bull market. It was also confirmed by another spike surge beginning in late December and culminating in a double ADS high in early January at +627 and +646. That spike pair should have removed all doubt about being fully invested in the market. We don't get any stronger knocks on the head than a believe spike, three SPAR buy patterns, a model upgrade and then another pair of believe spikes—all in the space of three months. In such cases, even with double spikes, *the rule remains the same: Buy the second day after the first spike.* You cannot be certain there will be a market reaction. If there is, it merely reinforces the secondary buy rule: buy the next ADS reaction low. Don't wait for an oversold ADS because you'll undoubtedly buy higher in doing so. In January 1975 the secondary buy at point 2 was only slightly higher in the S&P than the first, and it was the last chance to get into this market at a reasonably low range, S&P 73. Note that even the next SPAR buy signal (a thrust) didn't come until February at S&P 80.4. Not to worry—a great deal remained of the bull market.

Figure 7–7 amplifies previous chart patterns. First, the July ADS low at around –550 was not a low risk one qualifier, but the following rising lows foreshadowed the September S&P bottom and the July ADS low was immediately followed by a SPAR buy signal, albeit an early one. Note also the unusually long divergence between the rising ADS and falling S&P from July through September. Furthermore, the December ADS rally from the spike low near –500 was followed by sharply rising lows and the +725 believe spikes in January 1976 (see Figure 7–8).

This is another great example of why the term *believe* fits these spikes so aptly, and why even minor market pullbacks must be immediately bought despite the evident deterioration in ADS. The ADS believe buy came on January 8, 1976, the second day after the spike, at S&P 94.6. The market didn't even slow down until February 4 at 101.9. The secondary spike buy came at the first ADS uptick on January 12 at S&P 96.3. (The SPAR buy was a "dip" in March at 100.9.) Tardy investors didn't get a "good" *market* pullback until June 1976 and even oversold reactions in ADS wouldn't have helped until May.

Why does ADS show such dramatic deterioration after spike highs when the broad market (S&P) is still strong? Remember what ADS measures: how *many* stocks are advancing, net and smoothed for trend. The S&P measures both the number of stocks rising and *how far* they're moving, based on their weighting in the S&P 500 Index. It's

**FIGURE 7–7    1975 ADS and Standard & Poor's 500**

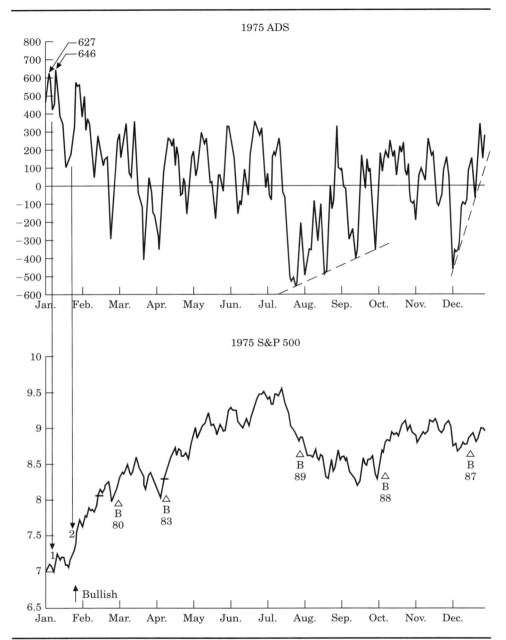

possible to have fewer stocks rising, but those that do so are rising smartly. That's what the apparent divergence in January–February 1976 reveals, but it is not the type of divergence that occurs in "developing" charts. Falling ADS lines that follow believe spikes are declining almost by default; they show that fewer stocks—perhaps preferreds and late stage cyclicals—are not able to continue rising day after day. Many may remain unchanged. But new leadership is emerging and those stock leaders are making decent moves. The S&P shows their power. Thus, a corollary can be added to our believe buy rule: when a

**FIGURE 7–8    1976 ADS and 1976 Standard & Poor's 500**

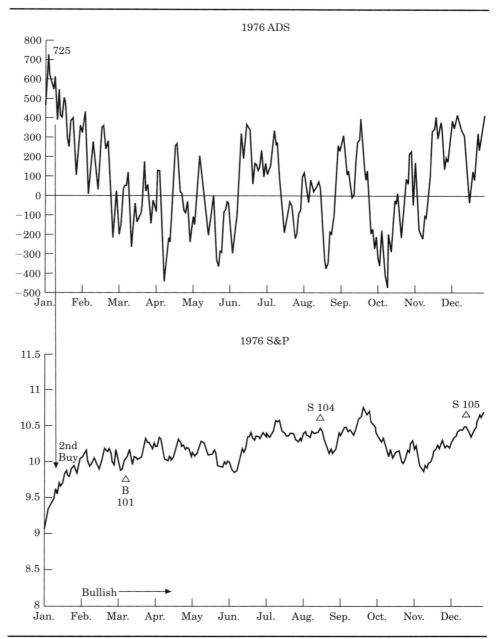

proper ADS believe formation appears, view any immediately declining ADs pattern as signaling only the temporary end of the market surge, not as a new declining developing pattern.

Consider also that the believe charts we've seen so far have occurred as the stock market was recovering from a bear market. Most other believe spikes came under similar conditions: August and October 1982, August 1984, February 1991 in the Persian Gulf War bear market recovery, and December 1991 after the black economic mood of the fall and November's overreacting market.

The next chart worth noting is the barn burner of 1982, which produced a rarity: two pairs of believe spikes (see Figure 7–9). This is the only year in the past two decades that the market has been so powerful that it produced two pairs of believe spikes in the same market run, one in August 1982 at +692 and +673, the other in October at +725 and +675. A SPAR buy pattern accompanied the initial rush, first on August 13 on a "dip" at S&P 103.9 (one day after the low), and a second, a major buy, on August 16 at 104.1.

**FIGURE 7–9    1982 ADS and 1982 Standard & Poor's 500**

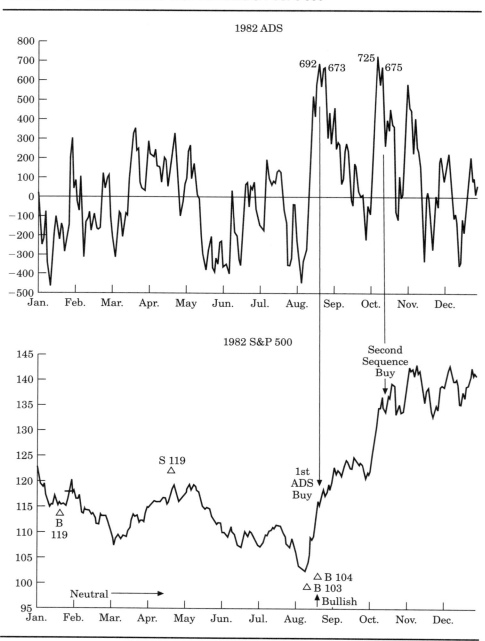

Our "get onboard" believe rules worked for the ADS chart. The primary buy came in the dip between the August spikes at S&P 117.6, and the secondary buy came at the first clear ADS drop following the second spike on August 30 at S&P 117.7. The market's first real rest started at S&P 124 on September 22.

In October 1982, the first spike came on the 11th, with the next-day ADS dip at S&P 134.4, if you could have caught it. The secondary buy came the second day after the next spike, on October 15 at 133.6. Remarkably, only the October 25 low at 133.2 and the November 23 low at 132.9 bettered that buy at any time in the decade thereafter!

The year 1991 proves as well as 1982 that when "believe" spikes occur even after major market moves, they should still be trusted (see Figure 7–10). The 1991 spike pair didn't arrive until February 6 and 11, with the S&P at 360 and 369, respectively. The low had been hit at 311.5 on January 8, with the Perian Gulf War rally starting on the 17th. Yet the primary spike buy rule came into force on February 8 and the secondary on the 13th. The horizontal line across the 1991 S&P 500 shows that these dips were still satisfactory buys throughout the year. Of course, SPAR itself signalled a thrust buy pattern the day the Persian Gulf War began, so it outproduced the ADS chart significantly. Still, ADS believe patterns did not let investors down.

We also must note that the second spike of the pair was a +617, just below the threshold qualification of +625. Technically, that spike would not have qualified. However, early February 1991 was still a fine time to buy small cap and secondary stocks, and the bull market that February's first spike confirmed had not ended at the time of this writing. Still, I rate such cases as merely close, and believe it is better not to chase them. If you do, be sure to use relatively close stops on issues or indexes purchased.

Confirming this reasoning, the December 1991 spike also missed qualification as a believe at another +617 reading. If traders had ignored this caution, they would have made a buy in early January 1992 at an S&P level that was near the high for six months. And they would have sustained a daily closing low nearly 6 percent below that in April. Not a serious blunder, but uncomfortable.

A riskier example is a sharp ADS spike that occurred in November 1977 and reached exactly +600. A buy after that would have caught the S&P near 96, a level that was barely exceeded by April 1978 with a bothersome 87 low in the interim.

While these important spikes approaching +625 appear to be significant as market powerhouse landmarks, they are not "believers." Their nonqualification implies an inability to sustain, which becomes more pronounced the farther below +625 they top out. Accordingly, I would treat all major ADS surges that fail believer qualification as just another ADS high that might become part of a downside developing pattern. These ADS surges are especially dangerous if they come during a rising developing pattern or following a strong gain in the S&P. (See also Statistical Notes, Part I.)

**FIGURE 7–10    1991 ADS and 1991 Standard & Poor's 500**

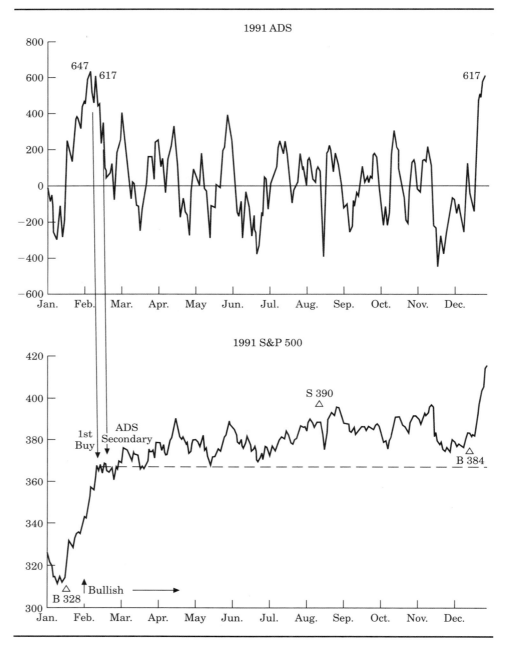

## "Believe" Formation Rules

Rules for believe formations are the simplest of all three types. When followed promptly, the rules can be highly rewarding.

**1.** When ADS crosses the +625 level, be alert for a believe pattern. Assume the market will head higher.

**2.** Buy the second day after the ADS high is set.

**3.** Because many believe patterns feature double spike highs, a second buy also may be made on the first market dip after a second high above +625.

**4.** Don't be surprised if a believe spike occurs after a major market rally has run a good distance like that of February 1991. That's in the nature of many powerful broad rallies. Obviously, risk is present at the higher levels and is probably greatest in the current market leaders. Consider the smaller caps at this time as well, but don't ignore qualified believe spikes.

Study Figures 7–11 through 7–17 illustrating ADS. You will probably discover other patterns that have some potential to forecast a trend or serve as a point of action. The types that I have just identified are the most reliable, so develop others with caution. Consider

**FIGURE 7–11    1972 ADS and 1972 Standard & Poor's 500**

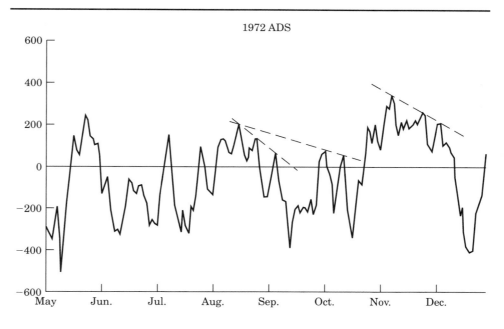

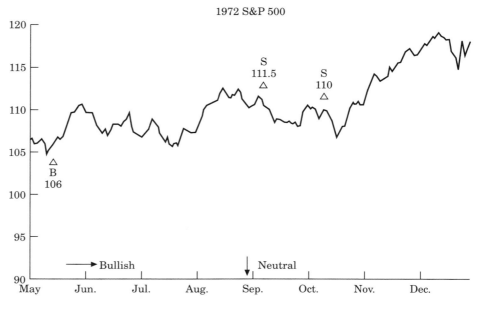

**FIGURE 7–12    1977 ADS and 1977 Standard & Poor's 500**

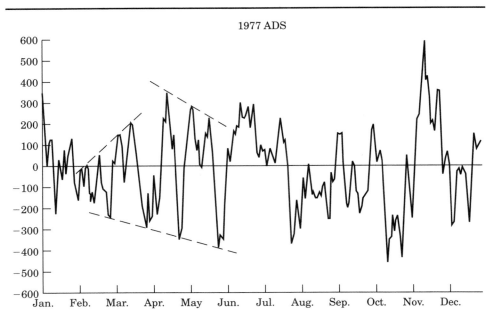

1977 ADS

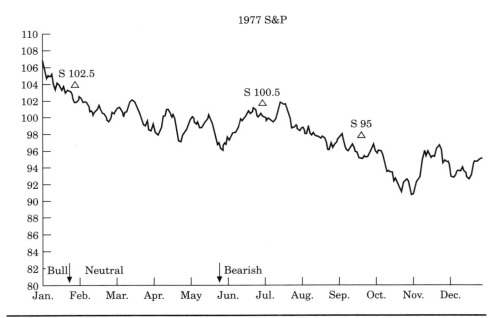

1977 S&P

the other patterns you spot as statistically weak if they make less than eight or 10 valid appearances. Even the believe category has only seven appearances.

What about the times when no clear historic ADS pattern appears, for example, mid-1992 and February through August 1993? The short answer is to be alert for a pattern to develop and don't try to force it into existence. There is no reason that some type of ADS pattern must exist at all times. It is when they do appear that counts.

**FIGURE 7–13    1979 ADS and 1979 Standard & Poor's 500**

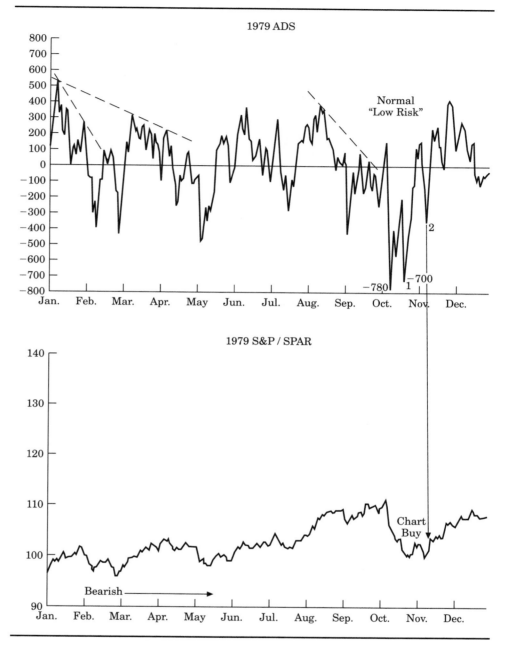

This again raises a point about SPAR. With short-term setup sells specifically, like that of January 1993, remember their double-edged quality and cast off the inapplicable reading when warranted. This is especially appropriate when no clear ADS pattern develops.

The chart analysis I have discussed depends on specific numerical levels. The –650 ADS level for low-risk types, +625 for believe types, and even the false breakout after two or more declining highs are arbitrary. These levels exist because they've worked, not because a theory demands them. Therefore, the specific numerical levels are more sus-

**FIGURE 7–14  1984 ADS and 1984 Standard & Poor's 500**

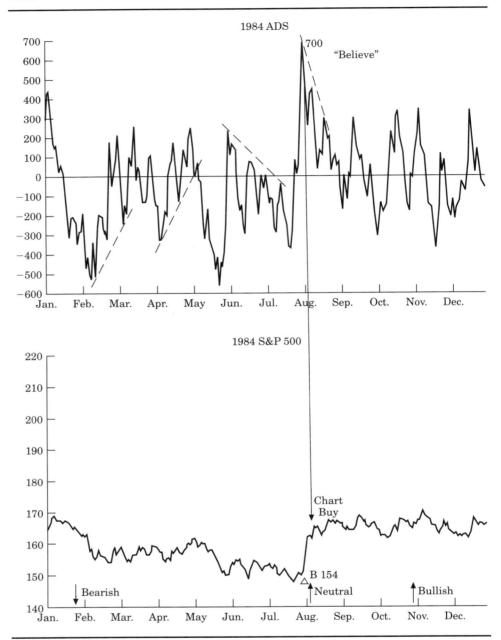

ceptible to change over time than the SPAR patterns themselves, which is the reason I searched out the latter. (See Statistical Notes, Part I.) Accordingly, use the ADS charts with caution and err on the side of missing a move. Better yet, use the charts in conjunction with other technical indicators as strong confirmations. There are many valuable insights in the ADS charts, but remember that change is the most permanent feature of the market. Contrarily, the SPAR patterns' mathematical precision, theoretical support, and lack of statistical randomness makes their potential longevity far more likely.

**FIGURE 7–15    1985 ADS and 1985 Standard & Poor's 500**

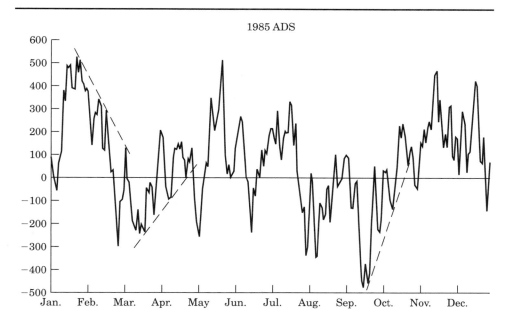

1985 ADS

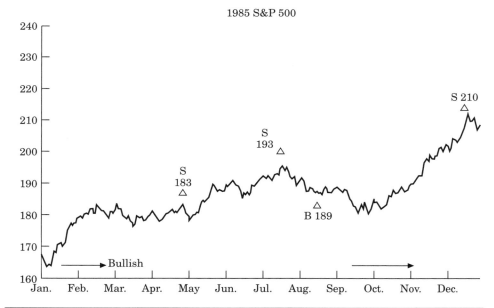

1985 S&P 500

**FIGURE 7–16    1988 ADS and 1988 Standard & Poor's 500**

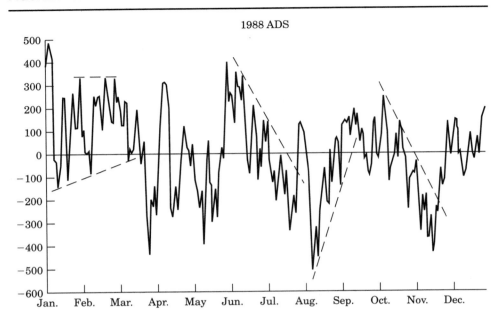

1988 ADS

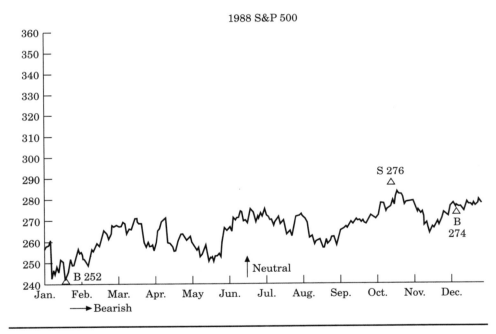

1988 S&P 500

**FIGURE 7–17    1993 ADS and 1993 Standard & Poor's 500**

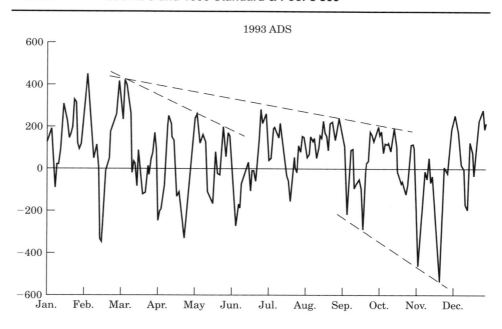

1993 ADS

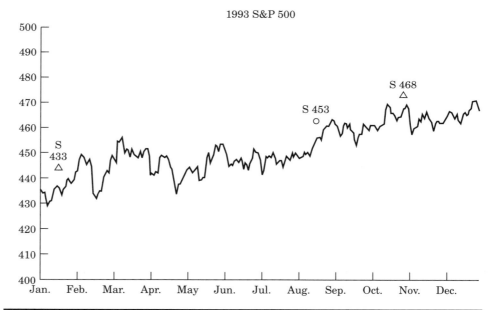

1993 S&P 500

**Author's Use Tip**

The extreme levels to which the ADS line occasionally moves are among the most reliable of all its chart formations. The real-time probem is allowing a given strong move *toward* an extreme level to finish its formation. With typical stock market variation, many starters will not finish. Or they will finish after a brief reversal. Since these chart forms are not inherent in SPAR, err on the side of waiting too long for their formation. If you miss one as a result, it is usually easy to recover by acting a bit late. SPAR will still guide you. But acting too early takes the serious risk of getting onto the wrong side of both SPAR and the market. Recovery from that is much more difficult.

# 8

# 1994 Update

The first half of 1994 provided an intriguing real-time test of the SPAR concept and a revealing insight into the interaction of SPAR and the Stock Model. As noted earlier, after three consecutive sell patterns in 1993 at succeedingly higher market levels, the average of which was a modest 3 percent from the year-end S&P mark of 466, SPAR entered the new year on a bearish note. However, the Stock Model remained steadfastly bullish with neither short-term interest rates nor market momentum hinting at the negative turns to come. Thus, the reading from the total system was that power money had been successfully selling into market strength through 1993 and had missed little on the upside. There was nothing yet on the market horizon to give cause for concern.

As the 1994 market rally rolled to new highs, SPAR's most common pattern, the stopper, appeared on January 19 for a brief three days with the S&P in the 474–475 area. This was 8 points, less than 2 percent, from the final high of 482. It would take eight sessions to reach that peak. This was also the third stopper to appear in 12 months. The others were February 5–11, 1993, and August 25–September 3, 1993, both of which included an interim market high that held for at least a month. (See Chapter 2, p.000 for the discussion of stoppers.) The important point to recall about stoppers is that the market rally *always* ceases for a time, typically one month, and it is subsequent market action that determines the long-term trend. In sum, by January 21, 1994, SPAR said the stage was set for another market pause of at least a month.

One assessment of SPAR's 12-month performance in late January 1994 might have been critical. SPAR seemed to have failed at getting things right. Higher market levels had followed each sell pattern, although a short-term correction had also taken place after all but the last stopper. (That was coming.) The market at the January 31 peak was 6.6 percent higher than the average 1993 sell, although only 3 percent above the previous one in October.

Aside from the fact that this criticism was about to be proven entirely erroneous by the market dive of March and April 1994, it reveals important misunderstandings of what SPAR was saying. First, it ignores the fact that SPAR's historic record was fully intact for calling market tops. Generating more than one consecutive sell pattern into a rising market was the hallmark of the 1973, 1977,

1980, and 1987 tops. The first sell of each period was several percentage points below the final peak, but the last in sequence averaged only a 4.0 percent miss over the past two decades. During 1993–94, SPAR was behaving normally. It didn't advertise that an *important* top was at hand. It had never done so before either. Market tops don't occur when "everyone" expects them.They come when buyers are driving the market higher, presumably in expectation of still higher prices ahead. January 1994 was no exception. Neither were SPAR's 1993–94 signals.

There are other problems with the critique. I've alluded to one, that of ignoring the success SPAR had in calling short-term results in each of its sell and stopper patterns. SPAR's sell signals are most successful in calling the market trend four to five weeks later. In each case during 1993–94, the sells were proven correct in this time frame. In fact, SPAR correctly forecast a market decline in the fifth trading week after a sell signal 19 of 24 times for its full 22-year record and 14 of 16 times in the out-sample period of pre-1984 and real time from June 1991. The probability of that success in the market occurring at random is 1 chance in 17,123 and 1 in 12,300 respectively. (See Statistical Notes, Part II.) SPAR was behaving normally in this way, too.

However, the key problem in thinking that SPAR was missing the boat in late January 1994 was in making the assumption that SPAR should signal correctly not only the short term, but also the medium and long term, or that it should forecast only important turns in the market. As we've seen, it patently does neither, nor does it even try.

To reiterate, SPAR tells us when power money is buying or selling. That's all it says. It speaks only when a previously successful buy or sell pattern is repeated. I believe that is important information because its track record is so remarkable. But to attach a non-stop rally or decline forecast to SPAR signals requires predictable timing. SPAR's timing is variable. For example, SPAR's sell record three months from signals is dramatically poorer than its fifth-week results: 12 of 24 correct for the full history and 9 of 16 correct in the out-sample. The odds of either of these being random are down to about 1 in 15, which is quite modest, but a far cry from less than 1 in 10,000+ seen in the fifth-week measure.

Interestingly, the SPAR sell record improves in the seventh month following a pattern appearance. The chances of that record being random rise to 1 in 91 in the full history, 1 in 333 for the out-sample. Thus, SPAR sell signals have very strong odds of not being random in the short term, mediocre odds in the medium term of three months, and again quite good odds in the seventh month. While the chances of SPAR patterns being random overall in a bullishly biased market (rising about 61 percent of the time) are very small, the basic 50 percent to 75 percent record of accuracy for a period ranging from one month to seven months is very sloppy for forecasting. That still doesn't diminish its value to investors, but it does make clear that forecasting is the waste of time that power money thinks it is. If you can achieve only a 3 percent to 7 percent error factor in selling into market tops as

SPAR has done over many years without forecasting the peaks, why bother with forecasts? That's just what SPAR was about to achieve again in January 1994. And it was doing so with its recent record intact: The three 1993 sells were all correct in their fifth week from appearance, they were all wrong at the three-month mark, and two of three were correct in the seventh-month range (May 1994 proved the latter).

There is still another facet to this: SPAR reversals of direction. In the 22 years through 1993, SPAR signalled a change of power money intentions within six months of a buy or sell pattern on just 14 occasions with an average time of three months. Yet, recall that the reversal was correct *every time* the next pattern appeared. Only once was the even initial pattern wrong at the date of reversal: The January 28, 1982, buy was reversed by a sell on April 23 for a loss of 0.25 percent. But that sell was correct to the tune of 12 percent at the August buys. So SPAR does reverse itself within six months about 25 percent of the time (14 of 58 total signals) and this makes all but short-term forecasting with SPAR difficult. But the reversals were the right steps to take. These facts clearly bolster the argument that forecasting is of little use with SPAR, but that doesn't harm the results.

The correct way to view SPAR's 12-month record in early 1994 was that it had been successfully performing its short-term function. It was typically off in the medium term. While the jury was still out on the long term, the probability was good for a market slump to occur between March and May 1994, the seventh months after the August and October 1993 sell patterns. Funny how things turned out.

Now let's bring the Stock Model into the picture. Throughout 1993 it was sturdily bullish, advising that the two critical market forces, interest rates and market momentum, were still on track and that investors should act mildly or moderately, not aggressively, on all SPAR sell patterns. The market responded with a continued upswing until January 31, 1994. Even at its closing low of 439 in the S&P 500 Index on April 4, 1994, it was not off 10 percent from that high. If we recall that the purpose of the Stock Model is to temper the degree to which we take SPAR signals—never to contradict them—it would seem that a fair appraisal of the 1993–94 SPAR–Stock Model interaction would award high marks.

We don't know the final story on the 1994 market correction. It may go much further or it may not. Given the amount of bearishness present by midyear, one might expect that further lows were ahead. SPAR disagreed. Following the first market correction after the Federal Reserve tightened credit on February 4, SPAR registered a dip *buy* pattern on February 8 at 471 on the S&P. Clearly, power money saw tighter credit as a mild problem and preferred to be on the buying side rather than the selling side. The official recommendation of SPAR was thus "buy on weakness." As of July, that buy appeared to be flat wrong. Was it?

Let's give this a closer analysis and not make the same mistakes that the January 1994 SPAR critique did. First, SPAR buys have an excellent 17 of 19 correct out-sample record at the fifth week following appearances (1 chance in 166 of being random). This time it missed by just two trading days, taking 27 days to exceed its buy level, not 20–25. At the three-month mark, the SPAR buy record drops slightly to 16 of 19 correct, but that's enough to drop the chance of randomness to 1 in 46. Again like sells, SPAR buys are not very efficient at this medium-term mark. It wasn't this year either, showing a loss of 4.9 percent. In sum, SPAR was again exhibiting normal behavior although with none too pleasing a trail.

The dip pattern appearance in February 1994 also had an unusual aspect to it. Among SPAR's four parameters, the short-term maximum line moved sharply higher just prior to the pattern date, going to an extreme level of 365. This SPAR component tracks short-term breadth strength or weakness and is the most sensitive to it. When this line rises sharply, it's saying that the market is getting overbought. But the dip buy pattern requires a market correction. The only way both events can occur near each other is on a sudden market drop that the short-term maximum line hasn't caught up with or is just beginning to. This is obviously a risky short-term moment to be buying and it was true in February.

The oddity is that only one other dip buy pattern of the prior 13 exhibited a steep short-term maximum line rise to an extreme level on the pattern day: July 30, 1975. That line had the same 71 percent brief prior rise as in February 1994, and it was followed by a sharp market decline of 7.5 percent in the S&P, similar to 1994. All other dip patterns showed *flat* short-term maximum lines except that of January 1986, but the amount of the rise then was mild, only 21 percent, not the 71 percent of February 1994. The market barely corrected in January 1986 following that dip pattern.

There is a strong temptation to say that we should not have bought on February 8, 1994, or that at least we should make that short-term maximum line test a part of the dip buy formula, given the coincidence of the two flawed occurrences and the dozen that all went on to higher markets. However, that would destroy our procedures for statistical randomness and cannot be done. Instead, in keeping with the dynamics of the SPAR concept, we'll take any future action on dip patterns with steep short-term maximum line rises only after a sufficient delay to ensure that an intermediate correction isn't around the corner. However, the point remains that the dip buy of February 1994 was displaying a peculiar internal quality.

The second aspect of the dip pattern's "buy weakness" advice is that it is ongoing. Until reversed by a sell, it says to buy on any worthwhile weakness in the market. The problem is how much is "worthwhile weakness"? SPAR does not give an answer. The degree of market weakness following the unusual dip buy in July 1975 suggested by this June that we had already seen the maximum extent of the 1994 market correction, about 7 percent from the signal, so any level below 471 in the S&P Index was a worthwhile buy. This is too facile. Instead, we may have better help from our ADS chart (see Figure 8–1.).

**Figure 8–1    1994 ADS**

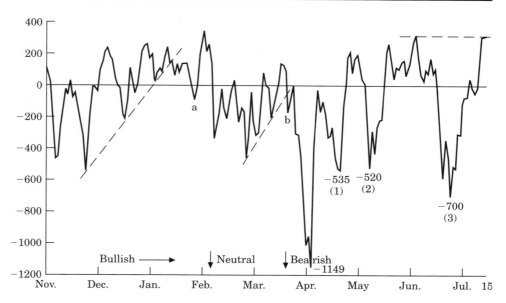

*Comments:* The rising lows from November 1993 to January 1994 formed a nice developing upside pattern complete with a false breakout at point *a*. The S&P 500 Index paralledled this, so the immediate correction was modest. During the second rising developing formation with its false breakout at point *b*, the S&P diverged. The S&P correction was significant. The June–July double top was in the reversal zone.

The rule is given in Chapter 7 under low-risk formations. Brought to 1994, the ADS low in April was –1149, but it was NOT made with a straight-line plunge from a positive level. The expectation was then for a complex low. With those, a trading buy is made only after the third rising ADS to follow, ignoring any interim lows above –200. That low was clear on June 28, two trading days after the –700 mark of the 24th was set. It followed interim lows of –520 on May 9 and –535 on April 20. A short-term "low-risk" buy was made on June 29 with the S&P at 447.6. The February and June buys were therefore profitable in the S&P by July 29 when the S&P stood at 458.

Next, the 1994 Stock Model deserves attention because it generated two downticks from its bullish stance of late January. The first downtick was to neutral with the interest rate hike on February 4, thus making the February 8 SPAR buy moderate, not aggressive. The second model move came on March 29 with the S&P futures break of the lower Bollinger band, which left the stock model outright bearish. This means that any future SPAR *sells* should be taken aggressively and any *buys* taken mildly until the model changes status. It is acting as a caution warning to any power money buying SPAR might spot.

As such, we now had the mirror reverse of 1993 in the SPAR–Stock Model interaction. SPAR was on a buy pattern and the model was bearish. Remember that when these two measures give opposite readings, as in 1993, it is not a contradiction on their part. The Stock Model is merely tempering SPAR action for prudence. The sum of their readings last year was that a market top was developing, but it was not likely to be a major one. In 1994 it became, there is risk in this market so be cautious and buy only on weakness, but there is little likelihood of a major downside move.

Again, neither the Stock Model nor SPAR was forecasting. They told us that in the fullness of time the right side of the market to be on is the long side, but it should not be chased. Through four months of 1994 that advice has been correct, with the market rallying 5.5 percent off its lows by June and reaching a high less than 2 percent below 471 in the S&P.

In the final SPAR event of 1994's first half, another stopper pattern appeared on June 15–16 with the S&P touching its rally high at 462. The immediate market reaction was to slump 4.3 percent and then bounce back 1 percent by July 1. It was another correct reaction from the market to a SPAR pattern.

Summed up, SPAR behaved normally in the first half of 1994, even allowing for the oddity in formation of the February buy pattern. It did this by showing no loss in the fifth week (plus two days) after the buy signal and showing one instead at the third month mark. SPAR had not quite reached the historical parallel of 1975 for the size of market correction following a dip buy signal, and it was just on the edge of its 5 percent to 6 percent "noise level." Its interaction with the Stock Model prevented the February buy from being aggressive. Moreover, with the three prior sell patterns, investor portfolios should have been cash rich by February, and a moderate buy should have retained sizable cash balances for the correction to come.

One could also argue that the stock market had overreacted to the worldwide bond market meltdown of March; without that, stocks would not have had the correction they did. When major companies like Procter & Gamble, Caterpillar, and Bankers Trust collectively lose over 300 million dollars on *mechanical* breakdowns in the bond/mortgage securities and derivatives markets,[1] a stock overreaction should be expected. With the market putting in higher lows during May and June than in April, this argument has credence.

Since we still don't know 1994's final market outcome, let us conclude that nothing had occurred by July 1994 that was outside SPAR's normal buy expectations. SPAR just "did its thing" through both 1993 and 1994, and those investors who expected only major turn signals from it were caught off base.

In mid-July 1994, the following SPAR system readings prevailed: (1) SPAR was still in its "buy weakness" mode, (2) the Stock Model was still in a high-risk attitude, (3) the ADS chart was revealing none of the three key formations discussed in Chapters 6 and 7, and (4) the S&P 500 Index had broken the November and September 1993 lows, but not the more prominent July and April/February 1993 marks.

My reading is that it will be worthwhile to buy market weakness ahead, according to the SPAR pattern. However, do so mildly, with mod-

---

[1]*The Wall Street Journal*, May 20, 1994

est capital and the retention of ample cash reserves according to the Stock Model, in this still uncertain, nontrending market per the ADS chart. Watch carefully for any new SPAR signal or a break that holds below the prior S&P lows of 439–441. Either could change the picture significantly and must be acted upon. And, remember that August 1994 is the seventh month following the February 8 SPAR buy. According to SPAR's history, the S&P should rise above 471 in this month.

# Conclusions

The complete SPAR strategy—system, if you wish—has been unfolded. It is clearly comprehensive, so much so that investors who follow it should have very few future days in the market without seeing a clear action picture.

This strategy is also unique. As one experienced investment manager put it, "there's nothing else like it out there." One reason for its unusualness is its distinct, separate segments, which I've described as modules. They operate totally independent of one another and thereby act as cross-checks on market pictures provided by each. These modules can be utilized separately, too, especially the SPAR patterns, but can also be used with any other strategy an investor has developed. When used in combination with each other, though, they provide a powerful interlocking strategy that makes clear when market positions can be safely increased and when they should be protected.

The SPAR patterns themselves have the distinct advantage of being inherent in, not superimposed upon the market. With them the maket itself tells the story. No interpretation of them is necessary, nor are outside indicators required, (except in the case of quantifying aggressiveness of action.) Proof is in their (1) excess return over the S&P 500 both historically and recently, (2) ability to position investors correctly for the market's major highs and lows, (3) statistical lack of randomness in appearances, and (4) multiyear real-time record that's remained well within its historical parameters of accuracy and market out-performance.

Perhaps most importantly, in the cautious-investor environment of the postcrash 90s, the strategy's non-pattern segments—the Stock Model, the short term timing and support refinements and the ADS formations—offer significant capital protection. They provide hard evidence that safety can be an integral part of a sound market game plan.

In summary, the SPAR strategy gives investors a complete set of market tools. Like any tool set, it doesn't all have to be used to get the job done. However, if all tools have been used throughout the enormously varied past two decades of market swings all the necessary work would have been accomplished with important protection against errors. That's a great deal to ask of any strategy. But I have no concern about asking it again for the future.

Simply put, SPAR patterns are sometimes early, but they're right.

# APPENDIXES

# *I* SPAR Buy and Sell Record, 1972–93

| All sells to first buys | | | All buys to first sells | | |
|---|---|---|---|---|---|
| Date | S&P | Gain | Date | S&P | Gain |
| 9/72 | 111.5 | | 5/72 | 106.4 | |
| Buy 10/74 | 65.0 | | Sell 9/72 | 111.5 | |
| | | 41.7% | | | 4.8% |
| | | | 10/74 | 65 | |
| 10/72 | 110 | | Sell 8/76 | 104.4 | |
| Buy 10/74 | 65.0 | | | | 60.6% |
| | | 40.9% | 10/74 | 71.2 | |
| 8/76 | 104.4 | | Sell 8/76 | 104.4 | |
| Buy 4/80 | 102.6 | | | | 47.5% |
| | | 1.7% | 12/74 | 67.3 | |
| 12/76 | 105.1 | | Sell 8/76 | 104.4 | |
| Buy 4/80 | 102.6 | | | | 55.1% |
| | | 2.4% | 2/75 | 80.4 | |
| 2/77 | 102.5 | | Sell 8/76 | 104.4 | |
| Buy 4/80 | 102.6 | | | | 24.9% |
| | | −0.1% | 4/75 | 83.8 | |
| 6/77 | 100.5 | | Sell 8/76 | 104.4 | |
| Buy 4/80 | 102.6 | | | | 24.6% |
| | | −2.1% | 7/75 | 88.8 | |
| 9/77 | 95.2 | | Sell 8/76 | 104.4 | |
| Buy 4/80 | 102.6 | | | | 17.6% |
| | | −7.8% | 12/75 | 87.8 | |
| 2/80 | 116.3 | | Sell 8/76 | 104.4 | |
| Buy 4/80 | 102.6 | | | | 18.9% |
| | | 11.7% | 12/75 | 87.8 | |
| 3/81 | 137.1 | | Sell 8/76 | 104.4 | |
| Buy 10/14 | 118.8 | | | | 18.9% |
| | | 13.3% | 3/76 | 100.9 | |
| 4/82 | 118.6 | | Sell 8/76 | 104.4 | |
| Buy 8/82 | 103.9 | | | | 3.4% |
| | | 12.4% | 4/80 | 102.6 | |
| 11/83 | 164.4 | | Sell 3/81 | 137.1 | |
| Buy 8/84 | 154.1 | | | | 33.6% |
| | | 6.3% | 8/80 | 122.4 | |
| 4/85 | 183.4 | | Sell 3/81 | 137.1 | |
| Buy 8/85 | 189 | | | | 12.0% |
| | | −3.1% | 10/81 | 118.8 | |
| 7/85 | 193.3 | | Sell 4/82 | 118.6 | |
| Buy 8/85 | 189 | | | | −0.2% |
| | | 2.2% | 1/82 | 118.9 | |
| 12/85 | 209.9 | | Sell 4/82 | 118.6 | |
| Buy 1/86 | 206.7 | | | | −0.3% |
| | | 1.5% | | | |

| All sells to first buys | | |
| --- | --- | --- |
| Date | S&P | Gain |
| 8/82 | 103.9 | |
| 3/87 | 294.1 | |
| Buy 11/87 | 230.2 | |
| | | 21.7% |
| 7/87 | 315.7 | |
| Buy 11/87 | 230.2 | |
| | | 27.1% |
| 10/88 | 276.4 | |
| Buy 11/88 | 273.7 | |
| | | 1.0% |
| 5/89 | 321.6 | |
| Buy 7/89 | 319.2 | |
| | | 0.7% |
| 7/90 | 365.4 | |
| Buy 10/90 | 314.9 | |
| | | 13.8% |
| 8/91 | 389.9 | |
| Buy 12/91 | 384.5 | |
| | | 1.4% |
| 6/92 | 410.3 | |
| Buy 6/92 | 408.1 | |
| | | 0.5% |
| 1/93 | 433 | |
| year-end | 466.5 | |
| | | −7.7% |
| 8/93 | 453 | |
| year-end | 466.5 | |
| | | −3.0% |
| 10/28 | 467.7 | |
| year-end | 466.5 | |
| | | 0.3% |

| All buys to first sells | | |
| --- | --- | --- |
| Date | S&P | Gain |
| Sell 11/83 | 164.4 | |
| | | 58.2% |
| 8/82 | 104.1 | |
| Sell 11/83 | 164.4 | |
| | | 58.0% |
| 6/83 | 162.6 | |
| Sell 11/83 | 164.4 | |
| | | 1.1% |
| 8/84 | 154.1 | |
| Sell 4/85 | 183.4 | |
| | | 19.0% |
| 8/85 | 189 | |
| Sell 12/85 | 209.9 | |
| | | 11.0% |
| 1/86 | 206.7 | |
| Sell 3/87 | 294.1 | |
| | | 42.3% |
| 4/86 | 233.5 | |
| Sell 3/87 | 294.1 | |
| | | 25.9% |
| 11/87 | 230.2 | |
| Sell 10/88 | 276.4 | |
| | | 20.1% |
| 1/88 | 252.1 | |
| Sell 10/88 | 276.4 | |
| | | 9.7% |
| 11/88 | 273.7 | |
| Sell 5/89 | 321.6 | |
| | | 17.5% |
| 2/89 | 287.8 | |
| Sell 5/89 | 321.6 | |
| | | 11.7% |
| 7/89 | 319.2 | |
| Sell 7/90 | 365.4 | |
| | | 14.5% |
| 10/89 | 340.3 | |
| Sell 7/90 | 365.4 | |
| | | 7.4% |
| 12/89 | 342.8 | |
| Sell 7/90 | 365.4 | |
| | | 6.6% |
| 5/90 | 338.4 | |
| Sell 7/90 | 365.4 | |
| | | 8.0% |
| 10/90 | 314.9 | |
| Sell 8/91 | 389.9 | |
| | | 23.8% |
| 10/90 | 304.7 | |
| Sell 8/91 | 389.9 | |
| | | 28.0% |
| 1/91 | 328 | |
| Sell 8/91 | 389.9 | |
| | | 18.9% |

| All sells to first buys | | | All buys to first sells | | |
|---|---|---|---|---|---|
| Date | S&P | Gain | Date | S&P | Gain |
| | | | 12/91 | 384.5 | |
| | | | Sell 1/93 | 433 | |
| | | | | | 12.6% |
| | | | 6/92 | 408.1 | |
| | | | Sell 1/93 | 433 | |
| | | | | | 6.1% |
| Average gain | | 7.4% | Average Gain | | 21.2% |
| Total Sells | 24 | | Total Buys | 34 | |
| Profitable | 16 | | Profitable | 32 | |
| Errors | 8 | | Errors | 2 | |
| | | | | | |
| Grand Total | 58 | | | | |
| Profitable | 48 | | | | |
| Errors | 10 | | | | |

See Statistical Notes, Part II for significance of this record.

# *II* Complete SPAR Track Record to Fixed Dates

| Date | Type | S&P | 1 Mo | 3 Mo | 6 Mo | Model@ Sig | Counts Buy 1 Mo. | 3 Mo. | 6 Mo. | Sell 1 Mo. | 3 Mo. | 6 Mo. | Both 7 Mo. |
|------|------|-----|------|------|------|------------|-----|-------|-------|-----|-------|-------|------|
| 5/12/72 | T-B | 106.4 | 107.1 + | 112.6 + | 115.1 + | Bullish | 1 | 1 | 1 | | | | 1 |
| 9/11 | SS | 111.5 | 109.9 + | 118.6 e | 110.5 + | Neutral | | | | 1 | 0 | 1 | 1 |
| 10/10 | SS | 110 | 113.4 e | 118.1 e | 112.2 e | Neutral | | | | 0 | 0 | 0 | 1 |
| 1973 no signals | | | | | | | | | | | | | |
| 10/7/74 | Mj-B | 65 | 73.1 + | 71.2 + | 85.6 + | Bearish | 1 | 1 | 1 | | | | 1 |
| 10/17 | W-B | 71.2 | 73.1 + | 70.7 e | 86.0 + | Neutral | 1 | 0 | 1 | | | | 1 |
| 12/10 | Mj-B | 67.3 | 71.2 + | 84.8 + | 90.6 + | Neutral | 1 | 1 | 1 | | | | 1 |
| 2/26/75 | D-B | 80.4 | 83.6 + | 91.2 + | 85.5 + | Bullish | 1 | 1 | 1 | | | | 1 |
| 4/10 | Mj-B | 83.8 | 89.6 + | 95.2 + | 89.3 + | Bullish | 1 | 1 | 1 | | | | 1 |
| 7/30 | D-B | 88.8 | 84.4 e | 89.3 + | 101.2 + | Bullish | 0 | 1 | 1 | | | | 1 |
| 12/4 | D-B | 87.8 | 92.6 + | 110.6 + | 99.6 + | Bullish | 1 | 1 | 1 | | | | 1 |
| 12/11 | Mj-B | 87.8 | 96.3 + | 100.9 + | 103.6 + | Bullish | 1 | 1 | 1 | | | | 1 |
| 3/16/76 | D-B | 100.9 | 101.1 + | 103.6 + | 106.3 + | Bullish | 1 | 1 | 1 | | | | 1 |
| 8/16 | SS | 104.4 | 103.9 + | 100.6 + | 100.5 + | Bullish | | | | 1 | 1 | 1 | 1 |
| 12/14 | LT-S | 105.1 | 103.4 + | 102.1 + | 100.4 + | Bullish | | | | 1 | 1 | 1 | 1 |
| 2/1/77 | SS | 102.5 | 100.4 + | 100.1 + | 98.1 + | Neutral | | | | 1 | 1 | 1 | 1 |
| 6/30 | LT-S | 100.5 | 99.1 + | 96.0 + | 91.6 + | Bearish | | | | 1 | 1 | 1 | 1 |
| 9/15 | SS | 95.2 | 93.5 + | 93.4 + | 89.5 + | Bearish | | | | 1 | 1 | 1 | 1 |
| 1978 no signals | | | | | | | | | | | | | |
| 1979 no signals | | | | | | | | | | | | | |
| 2/7/80 | SS | 116.3 | 106.9 + | 104.8 + | 123.3 e | Bearish | | | | 1 | 1 | 0 | 0 |
| 4/15 | W-B | 102.6 | 106.3 + | 121.4 + | 131.5 + | Bearish | 1 | 1 | 1 | | | | 1 |
| 8/29 | D-B | 122.4 | 123.5 + | 137.0 + | 131.1 + | Bullish | 1 | 1 | 1 | | | | 1 |
| 3/25/81 | LT-S | 137.1 | 133.9 + | 132.6 + | 115.9 + | Neutral | | | | 1 | 1 | 1 | 1 |
| 10/14 | W-B | 118.8 | 122.9 + | 117.2 e | 115.7 e | Bearish | 1 | 0 | 0 | | | | 0 |
| 1/28/82 | T-B | 118.9 | 113.1 e | 116.8 e | 106.4 e | Neutral | 0 | 0 | 0 | | | | 1 |
| 4/23 | O-S | 118.6 | 114.9 + | 109.4 + | 135.3 e | Neutral | | | | 1 | 1 | 0 | 0 |
| 8/13 | D-B | 103.9 | 122.2 + | 137.0 + | 147.6 + | Neutral | 1 | 1 | 1 | | | | 1 |
| 8/16 | Mj-B | 104.1 | + | + | + | Neutral | 1 | 1 | 1 | | | | 1 |
| 6/1/83 | D-B | 162.6 | 166.6 + | 164.2 + | 165.8 + | Bullish | 1 | 1 | 1 | | | | 1 |
| 11/10 | O-S | 164.4 | 165.1 e | 156.5 + | 156.6 + | Neutral | | | | 1 | 1 | 1 | 1 |
| 8/1/84 | T-B | 154.1 | 167.1 + | 167.5 + | 180.6 + | Bearish | 1 | 1 | 1 | | | | 1 |
| 4/25/85 | SS | 183.4 | 187.6 e | 189.6 e | 189.8 e | Bullish | | | | 0 | 0 | 0 | 0 |
| 7/12 | SS | 193.3 | 188.5 + | 186.1 + | 208.4 e | Bullish | | | | 1 | 1 | 0 | 0 |
| 7/19 | LT-S | 195.1 | (same seq not tracked) | | | | | | | | | | |
| 8/8 | D-B | 189 | 188.2 e | 197.3 + | 217.4 + | Bullish | 0 | 1 | 1 | | | | 1 |
| 12/13 | O-S | 209.9 | 206.6 + | 235.6 e | 247.6 e | Bullish | | | | 1 | 0 | 0 | 0 |
| 1/13/86 | D-B | 206.7 | 216.2 + | 242.2 + | 236.4 + | Bullish | 1 | 1 | 1 | | | | 1 |
| 4/8 | D-B | 233.5 | 237.2 + | 243.0 + | 235.5 + | Bullish | 1 | 1 | 1 | | | | 1 |
| 3/19/87 | SS | 294.1 | 286.9 + | 309.0 e | 321.2 e | Bullish | | | | 1 | 0 | 0 | 1 |
| 7/29 | SS | 315.7 | 334.6 e | 244.8 + | 255.6 + | Bearish | | | | 0 | 1 | 1 | 1 |
| 8/7 | LT-S | 323 same seq | | | | | | | | | | | |

| Date | Type | S&P | 1 Mo | 3 Mo | 6 Mo | Model@ Sig | Buy 1 Mo. | 3 Mo. | 6 Mo. | Sell 1 Mo. | 3 Mo. | 6 Mo. | Both 7 Mo. |
|------|------|-----|------|------|------|------------|-----------|-------|-------|------------|-------|-------|------------|
| 11/30 | W-B | 230.2 | 244.5 + | 267.9 + | 267.1 + | Bearish | 1 | 1 | 1 | | | | 1 |
| 1/15/88 | Mj-B | 252.1 | 257.6 + | 257.9 + | 266.7 + | Bearish | 1 | 1 | 1 | | | | 1 |
| 10/17 | SS | 276.4 | 267.7 + | 286.9 e | 308.7 e | Neutral | | | | 1 | 0 | 0 | 0 |
| 11/30 | T-B | 273.7 | 279.4 + | 294.8 + | 327.0 + | Neutral | 1 | 1 | 1 | | | | 1 |
| 2/27/89 | D-B | 287.8 | 291.6 + | 319.1 + | 344.7 + | Neutral | 1 | 1 | 1 | | | | 1 |
| 5/26 | SS | 321.6 | 326.6 e | 349.8 e | 346 e | Bullish | | | | 0 | 0 | 0 | 1 |
| 7/3 | D-B | 319.2 | 343.75 + | 356.94 + | 353.8 + | Bullish | 1 | 1 | 1 | | | | 1 |
| 10/31 | Mj-B | 340.4 | 343.6 + | 330.9 e | 342 + | Bullish | 1 | 0 | 1 | | | | 1 |
| 12/20 | D-B | 342.8 | 339.1 e | 337.6 e | 355.1 + | Bullish | 0 | 0 | 1 | | | | 1 |
| 5/4/90 | T-B | 338.3 | 367.4 + | 334.8 e | 306 e | Bullish | 1 | 1 | 0 | | | | 0 |
| 7/12 | O-S | 365.4 | 339.9 + | 300.0 + | 316.2 + | Bullish | | | | 1 | 1 | 1 | 1 |
| 10/1 | MJ-B | 314.9 | 301.8 e | 321.9 + | 378.7 + | Neutral | 0 | 1 | 1 | | | | 1 |
| 10/26 | W-B | 304.7 | 316.5 + | 340.91 + | 380.8 + | Neutral | 1 | 1 | 1 | | | | 1 |
| 1/17/91 | T-B | 327.9 | 364.2 + | 380.9 + | 387.6 + | Neutral | 1 | 1 | 1 | | | | 1 |
| 8/14 | SS | 389.9 | 387.3 + | 397.1 e | 407.4 e | Bullish | | | | 1 | 0 | 0 | 0 |
| 12/16 | T-B | 384.4 | 420.7 + | 409.8 + | 403.4 + | Bullish | 1 | 1 | 1 | | | | 1 |
| 6/15/92 | SS | 410.3 | 413.7 e | 419.9 e | 429.1 e | Bullish | | | | 0 | 0 | 0 | 0 |
| 6/30/92 | T-B | 408.1 | 422.2 + | 416.2 + | 435.7 + | Bullish | 1 | 1 | 1 | | | | 1 |
| 1/13/93 | SS | 433.0 | 446.2 e | 448.9 e | 447.3 e | Bullish | | | | 1 | 0 | 0 | 0 |
| 8/18 | O-S | 452.6 | 452.9 e | 460.2 e | 466.5 e | Bullish | | | | 1 | 0 | 0 | 1 |
| 10/28 | SS | 467.7 | 463.0 + | 481.6 e | 466.5 + | Bullish | | | | 1 | 0 | 1 | — |
| Yearend'93 | | 466.5 | | | | | | | | | | | |

Note: On last two sells, year-end 1993 is substituted for 6 mos.

*Summary*

| | 1 Mo. | 3 Mo. | 6 Mo. | 1 Mo. | 3 Mo. | 6 Mo. | 7 Mo. |
|--|--|--|--|--|--|--|--|
| Tot corr. | 29 | 29 | 31 | 19 | 12 | 11 | 46 |
| Tot Event | 34 | 34 | 34 | 24 | 24 | 24 | 57 |
| % | 85.3% | 85.3% | 91.2% | 79.0% | 50.0% | 4 5.8% | 80.7% |

| B&S days | 1 mo. | 3 mo. | 6 mo. | 7 mo. |
|--|--|--|--|--|
| correct | 48 | 41 | 42 | 46 |
| err | 10 | 17 | 16 | 11 |

Best comb: Buy 6 mo., sell 1 mo.= 48/58    82.8%
Worst comb: Buy 1 mo. or 3 mo., sell 6 mo. =40/57   70.2%

Key:

(1) The fixed dates shown, 1 month, 3 months, etc., are measured in trading sessions after signal date. 1 month = 20–25 sessions, 3 months = 65–70 sessions, 6 months = 125–130 sessions. Only the last column, seventh month, uses a full trading month as the measurement period.

(2) Type of signal: T-B = thrust buy, Mj-B = major buy, D-B = dip buy, W-B = waterfall buy, SS = setup sell, LT-S = long term sell, O-S = ordinary sell.

(3) The + or e after the S/P levels = + correct, e-error.

*Appendix*

# *III* Statistical Notes

## I. Fixed numbers

Stock Pattern Recognition uses certain fixed numbers as trigger points. These include the preconditions for buy and sell patterns in the SPAR absolute line and in the Advance-Decline Smoothed (ADS) line. I am aware that this presents something of a statistical problem. The number of issues traded on the New York Stock Exchange (NYSE) has increased dramatically over the two decades of SPAR history. To the extent that this increase provides more net declines in sharp market drops and more net gainers in sharp rises, any fixed number used as a trigger level will become easier to hit. For example, in the five years from 1989 through 1993 average advances and declines during the last five trading days of the year, a typically active period, went from 1,490 to 2,068 per day, an increase of 39 percent. This was an unusually productive time for new NYSE listings, however. From the same period in 1980, average advances/declines *declined* from 1,582 to the 1,490 level in 1989. The latter is close to the average of 1,470 for 1972–78. Of course, any single year might be an aberration. I'm talking about a trend and the recent activity trend is up.

It also must be noted that while the number of active issues in the last period has clearly risen, we cannot be certain that they either did or will exaggerate trends by appearing in similar numbers as *net* advances or declines. During the 1990s, a large number of foreign issues and bond funds were listed on the NYSE. Depending on the cause of a given advance-decline balance, these issues may or may not participate. We can't generalize their inclusion. For example, gainers and losers increased from 1,566 during the year-end period of 1987 to 2,066 at year-end 1993, but the extremes reached by the ADS line during the crash on October 19, 1987, and the April 4, 1994 bond market meltdown were only 15 issues apart—both in the −1,150 area. Moreover, an ADS negative extreme of −911 occurred in October 1978 and so did another one of −910 in October 1990. Positive extremes in the range of +700 to +725 came in January 1976, October 1982, and August 1984. The best positive reading since was +647 in January 1991. Somehow, at extreme ADS readings the evidence is slim that increased numbers of gainers or losers have a material effect on our smoothed advance-decline line, and thereby, on the absolute line that is derived from it.

Nevertheless, a change in the future cannot be ruled out. For this reason, an adjustment for the advance-decline activity trend may be useful as a cross-check on specific trigger numbers. The important points are the 550 prebuy trigger, the 415 presell trigger, and the two numbers used as triggers in the low-risk and "believe" chart analysis, −650 and 625, respectively.

The sample period during which the SPAR formulas were tested for effectiveness was January 1, 1984, through June 30, 1991. The tests were made using the above fixed numbers with fine success. This period then becomes the base for an average advance-decline index from which future changes will be applied. The index average for this period is 1,570 gainers and losers per day, based on year- end trading activity. Setting our important numbers as a ratio to the index we have:

$$550 \div 1570 = .35$$
$$415 \div 1570 = .26$$
$$-650 \div 1570 = -.41$$
$$625 \div 1570 = .40$$

These ratios must be held as constants for any new index reflecting changed advances and declines.

To smooth out abrupt changes, an arbitrary moving average of ten years made up of five-year groups is then obtained by dropping out the first five years of the sample and adding the most recent five-year average. Adding the 1989–93 daily average of 1,774 to the 1984–88 average of 1535 yields a new average of 1,655 to which the ratios can be applied. This provides the substitute numbers for the above fixed marks:

$$550 = 579$$
$$415 = 393*$$
$$-650 = -685$$
$$625 = 662$$

I have tested these numbers with the SPAR patterns and ADS ranges for the 12 months from June 1993 through June 1994. They made no difference in either the signals generated or the single low-risk chart formation of spring 1994. All events with the new triggers occurred at the same times without the adjustments. This might well have been expected for two reasons. The new trigger numbers are not much different from their original levels −20 −40 points—and the extremes of both the ADS ranges and the SPAR absolute line are far greater than either the old or new trigger numbers. In 1994 alone, for example, the ADS line ranged from −1,150 to +359 and the absolute line from 243 to 1,293. The new low-risk pattern trigger of −685 and buy trigger of 579 are in the area of one-half the applicable extreme. The daily numbers can move through the old or new triggers with ease. Moreover, since any increased numbers of NYSE advances and declines are likely to be felt when ADS or the absolute levels are changing rapidly (remember these are net numbers), it follows that the lines will then move through their triggers rapidly and a difference of 20 to 40 in the trigger levels will be truly inconsequential. Only when the daily net numbers of advances and declines are relatively small but in a trend can the new triggers be tripped on different days from the old numbers. That certainly could happen in the future, but not in the past year.

For your use in calculating new moving averages the current average is made up thus:

| Five-year Groups | | Individual Years | |
|---|---|---|---|
| 1984–88: | 1535 | 1991: | 1768 |
| | | 1992: | 1786 |
| 1989–93: | 1774 | 1993: | 2066 |
| Total | 3309/2 = 1654.5 rounded to 1655. | | |

When the 1994 activity number is available, it will be added and the 1984 number (1475) will be dropped and a new average calculated. By holding the original ratios above as constants, new numerators in the trigger number/new index side of the equation are calculated and applied in the formulas. They can then be used as cross-checks to the original formulas.

---

## II. Randomness

A significant point has been made about the lack of randomness in the SPAR pattern appearances. Randomness is the most serious statistical test that can be applied to any set of events because statistics does not allow conclusions of certainty to be drawn. One can never say that the success of a series of events means that the events will be certain or even extremely likely to repeat that success. However, by testing the success of an event for randomness, we can draw the strongest conclusion possible that its success permits. The closer the series of events is to being random, the less significant the series is, and vice versa. SPAR's lack of randomness is at an extremely significant level.

The test developed for randomness is the binomial distribution. It is calculated from the formula $(n!/(k!*(n-k!))(p\hat{\ }k)(1-p)\hat{\ }n-k$, where $n$ = number of observed events, $k$ = number of correct, and $p$ = probability of success of a random event in that environment.

Using the period of our original testing of the SPAR formulas—January 1, 1984, through June 30, 1991—the probability that the S&P 500 alone would rise from the end of one month to the end of the next

---

*The percentage change from 1570 to 1655, 5.4%, is subtracted here because the trigger occurs with a downward move in the absolute lien.

was 61.1 percent. The chance it would decline was the reciprocal, 38.9 percent. Thus, $p = 0.611$ in the equation.

This equation can now be applied to any series of independent events in the stock market. With SPAR, it is applied to each of the time and event parameters chosen to measure SPAR's success. This means buy to sell; sell to buy; buys to one, three, and seventh months later; and sells to the same periods. Statistically, it is incorrect to use the test sample period in determining SPAR randomness because the data are tainted by the testing and development of SPAR. Therefore, an "out-sample" period is the more valid for random determinations. In SPAR's case, that period covers from May 1972 to January 1984 and July 1991 through December 1993. Test results from this period are shown below.

## Buys

Buy to next sell: 17 of 19 correct.

Binomial coefficient: .005977
Chance of random: 1 in 167

Buy to one month: 17 of 19, same as above.
Buy to three months: 16 of 19 correct.

Coefficient: .0216
Chance of random: 1 in 46

Buy to seventh month: 17 of 19, same as first.

## Sells

Sell to next buy: 10 of 15 correct.

Coefficient .02033
Chance of random: 1 in 50

Sell to one month: 14 of 16 correct.

Coefficient .0000813
Chance of random 1 in 12,300

Sell to three months: 9 of 16 correct.

Coefficient .0741
Chance of random 1 in 18

Sell to seventh month: 12 of 16 correct.

Coefficient .003042
Chance of random 1 in 333

As long as each buy is unrelated to and independent of each sell and the buy periods don't overlap the sell periods (there were three), the combined success of all buys and sells and periods is the *product* of the coefficients of each period tested in a stock market that is modestly (61.1 percent) biased to the upside.

Buys and sells to first opposite pattern: .0001215,
one chance in 8,230.

Buys/sells to one month: 3.54E –06,
one chance in 2,057,613.

Buys/sells to three months: .0016,
one chance in 625.

Buys/sells to seventh month: 1.82E –05,
one chance in 54,945.

It is not possible to combine all results into a single number because the independence factor would be lost. Nevertheless, the range of results is dramatic. As noted at the end of Chapter 4, the closest chance of the buys and sells being random occurs at three months time, 1 in 625. The furthest chance is at one month, when the odds rise to a staggering 1 in 2 million+.

As shown, the chance of randomness for any one buy or sell in any period is far less than the combinations. Indeed, those that have less than 1 chance in 20 are statistically insignificant while those above 1 in 100 are important. Therefore, those that are statistically less important (less than 1 chance in 100 of randomness) are the sells to first buys, and both buys and sells at three months time. Only the sell to three months measure is statistically insignificant, where a larger sample might result in an essentially random reading. From the statistical standpoint, however, the entire SPAR out-sample is sufficiently significant to pose a serious question to the efficient market theory: Why do these patterns appear with such success? Adding further real-time and out-sample data and relating SPAR concepts to recent academic work that has cast some doubt on the efficient market theory is a future research step.

# Index

# INDEX